Peter Alliss was born into golf. The height of his playing
career came in 1958, when he won the Italian, Spanish and
Portuguese Opens in three successive weeks. Today, he is
the doyen of golf commentators and as such is regarded as
the rightful heir to Henry Longhurst. His television
programmes *Around with Alliss* and *Pro-Celebrity Golf*
are the most popular of their kind. His previous books
include *Bedside Golf* and *An Autobiography,* both
available in Fontana.

Peter Alliss
BEDSIDE More GOLF

ILLUSTRATIONS BY COLIN WHITTOCK

Fontana/Collins

First published by William Collins Sons & Co. Ltd 1982
First issued in Fontana Paperbacks 1984

Copyright © in text Peter Alliss 1982
Copyright © in drawings Colin Whittock 1982

Editor Michael Leitch
Designed by David Pocknell's Company Ltd
Production Reynolds Clark Associates Ltd

Made by Lennard Books
Mackerye End
Harpenden
Herts AL5 5DR

Printed and bound in Great Britain by
William Collins Sons & Co. Ltd, Glasgow

Contents

Preface

elcome to another Round and About with Alliss. Another collection of tales, some even true, from the Fairways and Bunkers of Life. A player once said, 'It's a funny game,' to which his ancient Scottish caddie replied, 'Aye, but it's no' meant to be.' Well, that's his opinion. For me, it's a game to be played with fresh air in your lungs and joy in your heart. I hope this new offering, gathered from the world's locker-rooms and caddie-masters' huts, will bring you joy, bridging those golfless gaps when the snow is thick on the ground, or there's been a power cut at your local driving range, and the next best thing to playing golf is reading about it ... maybe dreaming a little, too, about the next time ... how marvellous it's going to be.

The Story of Golf

t Gleneagles it's the birds. Woodpeckers, most of all. Ah, you think, how nice to be in these rich woodlands and hear the tap-tap-tapping of a woodpecker. Can't be much wrong in a world where you are in whistling distance of a cheery woodpecker, lightly drilling a tree-trunk for some of those tasty wood-boring insects, then flapping off through the silent air to other hunting grounds with that characteristic cry: 'Kik. Kik. Kik.'

It drives the sound men potty. 'Rat-tat-tat-tat! Blasted little Maschinenpistols. Strangle the lot.' The sound men are deaf to your defence of wild creatures in their rightful habitats. 'Ruined the whole sequence,' is all they'll say. 'Have to do it again.'

At Royal St George's it's the skylarks. Everywhere in the world there's something to put some member of a film crew into hysterical orbit. A hair in the gate, for example. Hairs in the gate are far worse than having the commentator stretchered off with bubonic plague. Once a hair appears on the film, magnified to look like the Grand Canyon, the whole sequence is wrecked; back you must go, and reshoot it. Or you may have a duff batch of film. You shoot the lot and nothing comes out. Marvellous. In the pure terms in which television people see things, that's worth at least three commentators struck with The Pest. And airports. Airports even have a machine – the x-ray machine that scans your body and your baggage – which can turn at least one make of film yellow. You might as well stay in Heathrow, the way that film's going to turn out. Only thing is, of course: you don't know. Yet. So, in the meantime, off you go to Japan, all waves and smiles; back, via Hong Kong and Calcutta, with miles of footage you can never use.

The Great Golf Rush

As a golf man first, and a television man some way second, I had been conscious of these technical problems for some time, but not over-concerned about them. Then I became involved in making the BBC series *The World of Golf*.

It took just over a year to put together – though the first talks began in 1979. Here, suddenly, instead of a half-hour or 50-minute film of one event, golf was being treated as a major undertaking, with a seven-week series about the entire history of the game. Both the subject and our approach to it were vastly more demanding than any single project I had tackled before. This was 'total' television.

I still find it bewildering to look at how golf has taken off as a television sport. Eight or so years ago, the pattern was to televise four or five tournaments a year, plus two or three special events such as The Big Three playing the best eighteen holes of golf. And that was it. Now golf is rarely off the screen; winter as well as summer. Of the programmes I am involved with – *Pro-Celebrity, Around With Alliss, Men v Women*, etc – I recently worked out that, in a twelve-month period starting with the run-up to Christmas 1981, there would be 42 going out – and that's before we get to 'the golf', the harder stuff of tournament play. It's been a quite remarkable explosion.

Credit for the *World of Golf* series rests with Gordon Menzies, a senior television producer with BBC Scotland. The idea was his, and for some while he took it round without success. But he stuck with it because he thought the concept was right, and eventually this started to register in the right places. In 1980 the series was accepted by BBC1 and Television Enterprises as a project to support, and work at last began in early 1981.

It's as well that Gordon Menzies has a strong competitive streak, because in these hard times it becomes that much more difficult to push through the budget for something as big as a seven-part series. But Gordon managed to get his budget after some tricky bits of cost-cutting – for example, sharing our camera crew with *The Money Programme* when we went to the Far East, and generally horse-trading with airlines and hotels everywhere. The first scripts were written in February 1981, and the following month we began filming.

Early Days

In the course of the next twelve months we went virtually everywhere that golf has taken root. Episode One, in terms of the finished programmes, deals with the origins of the game in Scotland. Since it seems to be a law of film-making that you never actually do things in their intended order, our first piece of film was shot at the US Masters in Augusta; but we'll come to that in a moment.

At home, it was a fascinating experience to go to all the old clubs – to Royal Blackheath, the Honourable Company of Edinburgh Golfers at Muirfield, to Old Prestwick and Musselburgh, and, of course, to St Andrews, and to delve into the great rivalry between these clubs over which was really first. What's extraordinary about this is how little was recorded in the early days – the very early days, that is, back in the time of James I. One of the reasons for this, I found, was that most of the early clubs were formed by masons. By definition, masons are a secretive lot, and matches were arranged on the very informal basis of private wagering. Who then beat whom and carried off the guineas was not for public consumption, so very few records were kept of early matches.

Something of this spirit survives at Muirfield. We filmed a dinner there, which was the occasion used by the members to fix up their matches for the next year. Out came the diaries, and all the Sundays were magically filled. There was no discussion of handicaps; it was all done, as it were, by ear. 'You and I are about level with him. So we'll play him plus A.N. Other.' And that seems to have been how the wagers were struck in the early days.

America Gets the Bug

We also chased up some other theories about the origins of golf: that the Ancient Romans began it with their *paganica*, using a bent stick to hit a feathery ball (or was it a slave's skull filled with sand?); that the Dutch began it with their *kolven* or *kolf*, which they sometimes played on ice but which was mostly played in a walled court, the object being to strike a post with your ball. Quite close, but not close enough. In the end, Scots will be relieved to hear, we gave Scotland the credit for being the true home of golf.

10

Then we went across to the United States. Here, too, the Scots were the driving force, emigrating there in large numbers in the late 19th century and encouraging the spread of the game at such a rate that, within a few years, America had a million golfers. The first courses were built around farms in Upper New York State, and we filmed at the very first club, the St Andrews Golf Club of Yonkers. This was founded in November 1888 by a Scot, John Reid, who laid out part of his cow pasture with three holes, playing on it with neighbours and friends. They expanded to six holes, then took over an apple orchard. Eventually, in 1897, they settled in their present home at Mount Hope, Westchester County.

We filmed at some other old courses and went to the headquarters of the United States Golf Association, at Far Hills, New Jersey, which was set up in 1894, the year before the first Open, Amateur and Ladies' Championships began. We took our cameras to Pinehurst, North Carolina, where the North and South Amateur Championships are held each year; we went down to Dallas to see Byron Nelson, and we covered the US Open at Merion, Pennsylvania, and the Walker Cup at Cypress Point in the spectacular Monterey peninsula in California.

By then, of course, we were looking at a game transformed into a huge industry. In fact, some years ago golf was rated the twelfth biggest business in the States. An amazing statistic, but with all the equipment – the clubs, the socks, the gloves, and so on – golf *has* climbed to almost unbelievable heights. We followed that track to Japan, where they have those extraordinary driving ranges. The Shiba, in Tokyo, has three levels and something like 155 bays, and the place is crammed with people cracking balls throughout the day and night.

KAMIKAZE
BALL COLLECTION
SERVICE

13

Some of these people will never get on a golf course. The driving range *is* their golf. The funny thing is, the Shiba actually has a great golfing atmosphere. It's so contrived it's ridiculous, and perhaps the atmosphere gets to you by saturation alone. Certainly, you can't get away from golf the moment you step in the door.

From Reception you look out onto a pair of attractive little putting greens. There's a large room with a monster television set that shows golf films all the time. You walk past the restaurant to Golf Reception, and there are the bays, dozens and dozens of them, wired in. Not that your average man can just arrive, pick up his bucket of balls and go off to play. He may have to wait two hours to get on.

Still, he can take his time. He's got all his immaculate golfing gear to change into, leaving his everyday clothes in a locker. If he has any opinion of himself at all, he will have bought all the latest in golf shoes, gloves, hats, sweaters, not to speak of his fine *full* set of clubs. It's almost surreal. Already that day we'd been to the famous Okachimachi open-air market in Tokyo, and counted more than thirty golf shops, all filled with the most staggering amount of stuff. There was not a thing you could possibly want for.

Any desire we may have had to load up with new gear was soon extinguished by the demands of our hectic, congested schedule. To give an idea of how much we had to cover – which means not just getting there, but setting up, filming, reshooting if necessary, packing up, on to the next place, plus eating, sleeping, etc – here is the timetable for our stay in Japan:

11 November 1645 Leave Hong Kong *2115* Arrive Tokyo (Narita Airport) Minibus to Hotel *2315* Meet Sho Tobari of Japanese Golf Association

12 November Honma Golf Factory, Yokohama; Hodogaya Country Club

13 November Okachimachi open air market; Shiba Driving Range; Japanese Golf Association Headquarters

14 November The construction of the new Seve Ballesteros Golf Club; Interiors of Sakura Golf Club; Helicopter coverage of same area

15 November Final day of the Toshiba Masters, near Mt Fuji

16 November Fly to Australia via Hong Kong

Who says it's a glamorous life?

Still on tour, we went to Hong Kong and Australia to look at some of the places in the old British Empire to which golf spread in the 19th century. India, too, did not escape the Scottish exiles, and in fact the two oldest golf clubs outside Scotland and England are the Royal Calcutta, founded in 1829, and the Royal Bombay (1842). We also took in the coastal developments in Spain, where golf is booming, visited two clubs in Madrid and covered the Spanish Open in Barcelona. By the time our travelling was done, there were few places left on the golfing map that we couldn't rightfully stick our BBC pin into.

ROYAL CALCUTTA
GOLF CLUB

LUNCHEON TODAY

CURRIED
HAGGIS

All-Time Greats

Time to think about players. We had two lists of all-time great players: first, the old-time greats, then the moderns. Gordon Menzies drew up the lists, and when I saw them I found it curious that it should be so difficult to disagree with his choice. But when you really get down to it, there is a very considerable gap between a great player and an all-time great. See what you think.

In the old-time list we had Harry Vardon, Walter Hagen, Bobby Jones, Gene Sarazen, Henry Cotton, Byron Nelson, Sam Snead, Ben Hogan, Bobby Locke and Peter Thomson. Our moderns were Arnold Palmer, Gary Player, Jack Nicklaus, Lee Trevino and Tom Watson.

We interviewed all the survivors on our list – except one. That was Ben Hogan who wrote us a perfectly agreeable letter but regretted that public appearances were not his thing. I respect his desire for privacy, of course, but have always thought that he had so much to offer the game it is a tragedy that he has decided to keep himself to himself. He goes daily to his club, so I hear, but only his close friends see Ben Hogan play. To the rest of the world he remains almost a recluse. Such a pity.

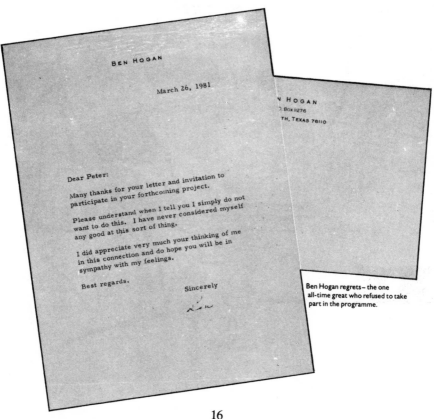

BEN HOGAN

March 26, 1981

N HOGAN
). Box 11276
TH, TEXAS 76110

Dear Peter:

Many thanks for your letter and invitation to participate in your forthcoming project.

Please understand when I tell you I simply do not want to do this. I have never considered myself any good at this sort of thing.

I did appreciate very much your thinking of me in this connection and do hope you will be in sympathy with my feelings.

Best regards.

Sincerely

Ben Hogan regrets– the one all-time great who refused to take part in the programme.

Women in Golf

The attitudes facing Catherine Lacoste, when she went over to the United States to play in the Women's Open and the Ladies' Championships, were forbidding to say the least. 'What does a Frenchwoman know about golf?' 'Who does she think she is?' 'Why doesn't she play to her strength – and get back to the cuisine?' That kind of thing. When she actually took the titles, in 1967 and 1969, there was an epidemic of moral outrage among her hosts.

In our programme on the rise of women's golf, we had an interview with Catherine Lacoste, now De Prado, in which she recaptured the animosity that greeted her triumph. It was a very strange episode, but then Americans *are* protective about their own national events – they don't like foreigners winning; the same thing has been happening to Seve Ballesteros, though if he goes on winning tournaments over there I suspect they'll just quietly adopt him in the end, pretend he's really some kind of Puerto Rican.

When the women's tour began in the United States, in 1946, there was no need for any of that flag-waving. The three top women – Babe Zaharias, Louise Suggs, Patty Berg – were American, and the tour itself was about as strong in terms of quality as it's ever been. In terms of size it was very much smaller than today, but given a launch of that quality it's hardly surprising that the women's game should have grown as it has done. It's only in the last five years that it has really made the big time, but today there's no doubt that women golfers can be very wealthy indeed, as we found when we filmed at the Lady Keystone Open in the chocolate town of Hershey, Pennsylvania. We chatted to Kathy Whitworth, who has already earned over a million dollars on the tour, and to Jo-Anne Carner who is only a few dollars short of the magic million. We also had a very interesting and frank conversation with Nancy Lopez-Melton, the biggest name in ladies' golf, about the strains and stresses of golf and marriage.

There's a close parallel between golf in the post-war period, especially in the last eight or ten years, and my own expectations of what golf would mean to me. It still seems about the day before yesterday that my best hopes were to carry on being a golf professional for as long as I decently could, and retire. Then came one or two offers of television work. Ah, I thought, interesting, might get a few hundred quid out of this. Instead, everything has mushroomed and we've reached the extraordinary situation, as I mentioned earlier, where the BBC are putting out 42 golf programmes a year which strictly aren't what the crustier viewers refer to as 'proper golf'. Then you get the 'proper golf', with more and more tournaments being televised all over the world, if necessary beamed by satellite so you can watch it with your late-night cocoa. Next we'll be having Breakfast Golf. Now *that's* a good idea. Must just go and give someone a ring . . . .

So You Think You Can Putt

ritical spectating begins even earlier in life now we have the gift of TV. And of all the topics people write in about, none is more popular than a particular favourite of mine – putting. So it was entirely fitting that C. Bourne of Eridge, Tunbridge Wells, should write to point out what he considered was a shady putt. He said he thought Hale Irwin cheated, because 'when he putts he pushes the ball half the way to the hole. I am glad that he did not win the Open. Thank you for the lovely commentry. C. Bourne (age 12).'

With the letter came a drawing. In it, a clearly bespectacled golfer in black sweater and blue plaid slacks labelled 'Hale Irwin' has just struck a golf ball with a motion labelled 'Push'. (Proof enough, you might say.) Watching 'Hale Irwin' from the edge of the page is a leering figure with a cheroot sticking from his mouth labelled 'Severiano Ballesteros'. Despite this double testimony, I replied that Mr Irwin wasn't cheating, that a 'push' was when there was no backswing at all and the ball remained on the face of the putter virtually throughout the stroke. So, although the Irwin action may have seemed a little suspicious, all was above board. I might have added that Severiano Ballesteros really ought not to puff cigars while out on the course!

PRACTICE GREEN

18

Next, and briefly, a regular correspondent from St Andrews has been trying to win me to his patent putting method. 'How would you like to be stone dead at six feet,' he writes, 'never take three putts again, and hole three times your fair share of 15-footers? How many Opens could you still win?'

Not many, was my first reaction, if three million others are in on the secret. Uncharitable perhaps, but there was something about the appearance of his letter – all dots, dashes and underlinings – that made me think he wouldn't have kept the world about him in the dark while he leaked the divine inspiration to me alone. It then turned out that the spark of his inspiration had been lit in 1948 (!) while watching Henry Cotton in the Spalding tournament. Henry, apparently, was having a lot of success addressing the ball off the toe of his putter. ... Ah, but I mustn't let on. Chap wants to train up his son and then, when he's ready, scoop the jackpot, winning Opens at will, international fame, fabulous wealth, sun tan all the year round. Can't blame a chap for dreaming. Better pass on to Sunny Cleethorpes.

Across the Slope

They have their own way of doing things in South Humberside, and I am grateful to Mr D. Ramsay, formerly the pro at Cleethorpes GC, for this little exercise in scientific putting. It was one of several competitions they held at Cleethorpes on Captain's Day, and neatly illustrates some of the problems posed by pace and borrow.

First, you cut a hole on a pronounced slope, then you mark out with whitewash a small square as your 'teeing ground', some six feet from the hole. Then – the devilish bit – you almost block the route to the hole with three tee pegs, each projecting about one inch and set in the ground with just enough room for a golf ball to pass between. This gives you four quite different routes to the hole:

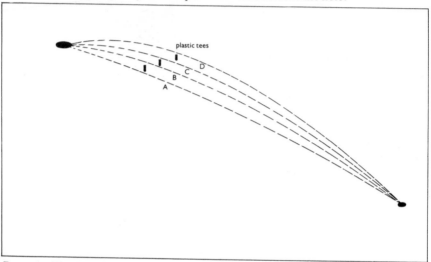

Route A   The Gary Player back-of-the-hole putt.
Route B   A little borrow but hit very firmly.
Route C   Medium borrow and medium pace.
Route D   For the connoisseur, a very slow putt with lots of borrow that just gets there and dies in the hole. 'Generally done by accident,' adds Mr Ramsay, 'and reminiscent of stymie days.'

Yes, indeed. We've all come to grief on that slippery slope. Of course, you can always loft the ball straight into the hole. That was the *dashing* way to beat a stymie.

Doctor, Doctor!

In my time as a player I was never renowned for being a great putter. I was all right in most departments, but thought to be a bit shaky on the greens, especially with those little three- and four-footers. It worried me a lot at the time, and one day I decided to visit a psychiatrist to see if he could smooth out my yips, or whatever.

He listened at some length to my problem, leaned back in his chair, fiddled with his leather blotter and said:

'The main trouble with you is your name.'

'My name?' I said.

'Yes, it's wrong for you. In your profession. It doesn't suit.'

'It didn't do my father any harm,' I pointed out.

'I'm talking to the son,' he said, pursing his lips. 'For you it's wrong.' Pause. More fiddling with the blotter. 'But listen,' he went on, 'you're lucky because there's something I can do. A man came in here and left me a deposit on a name, an

expensive name, and he hasn't come back to claim it. Now, I can let you have that name cheap, say for £500 if you give me your name in part exchange.'

'What's the name?' I asked.

'Goldberg.'

'Goldberg?'

'There you are,' he said, 'You're getting used to it already.'

I wasn't totally convinced, but agreed to take it on a week's trial. Frankly, it wasn't a huge success, and towards the end of the week I was counting the days. Exactly a week later I rang up the psychiatrist. His receptionist answered.

'Is Dr Lipschitz in, please?'

She said, 'We don't have any Dr Lipschitz.'

'Look,' I said, 'don't tell me you haven't got a Dr Lipschitz. I was in your office a week ago with him.'

'No,' she said, 'there's no Dr Lipschitz here. But we do have a Dr Peter Alliss.'

Danger! Golf in Progress

he warning sign will be familiar enough to visitors to the caddie master's shop at St Andrews. And for a certain lady in the White House there, no truer message was ever written. Her reactions on the fateful day when one Ted Lee came north from London, are enshrined in a poem, 'Incident on the Old Course'.

Lee had hit a sticky patch around the 11th hole, but by the time he reached the 18th tee his hopes of success in the Medal Round were rekindled. The poem goes on:

Under his slouched hat left and right
He glances and screws himself up tight,
Belly and bum and a followthrough
What man has done a man can do!

He hits the White House with a slice
And what he says is not quite nice,
He shatters a window with a crack –
With a lucky break the ball comes back

To land square on the field of play
Ted Lee thinks this must be his day!
But just as he takes his second shot
He knows good fortune is not his lot.

For out of the window a lady bent
And said in a voice of sad intent
'Shoot if you must at my coiffured head
But spare my wee White House!' she said.

Her cry quite undid Ted, obviously a chivalrous lad at heart. He pulled his next shot and finished in 91. But the window problem is something golfers have to be firm about. I remember down at Parkstone we had two big hitters, Vernon Haydon and Jack Santall. Vernon is actually in the *Golfer's Handbook* for long-driving feats and both men dearly loved to smash the ball.

The 5th hole at Parkstone goes alongside a road, over a bit of a hill with a lake

on the right-hand side. If the weather was very dry and conditions just right, you might possibly hit the green, but it needed a monster blow with the small ball.

These two gladiators, whose whole delight was slogging against each other, arrived at the 5th tee. Vernon gave it a pretty good thrash down the fairway, then it was Jack's go. He got up and gave his ball an almighty thump. Up it went, veered rapidly left, then Craash! Tinkle, tinkle. That unmistakeable sound. Jack put down another ball. Whoosh. Identical shot. Craash! More tinkle tinkle.

Fortunately he sliced his third one into the trees on the other side, but found it, and they carried on with their game. A few minutes later they were walking across the road to the 7th when they were confronted by a fierce-looking old lady, picking bits of glass and light bulb out of her hair. She glared at Vernon.

'It was you!' she yelled.

'I beg your pardon,' said Vernon, slipping on his innocent expression.

'It was you!' repeated the old lady. 'I know you! Hitting those balls all over the course.' She raised herself up like some headmistress about to demolish the entire school for misconduct. 'I was in the toilet! Suddenly your golf ball crashed through the window and ricochetted off the wall . . .'

Vernon and Jack were hard-pressed to contain themselves as they imagined the poor woman sitting in her loo, with a golf ball going bing-bong-bing-bong round the walls.

'Then another ball came in! Destroyed my light bulb! Of course it was you. Do you think I don't know?'

'Well, madam,' said Vernon, 'that's just not true. I hit a perfectly good shot down the fairway and Mr Santall put his ball into the trees on the other side.'

'Which *was* quite true,' said Vernon later. 'Except that I didn't tell her about Jack's two previous shots!'

Spectator Bashing

The most dangerous place to stand on a golf course is about thirty yards ahead of the tee on the player's left-hand side. If he drives over the top of the ball and catches it at the back of the club, then it will veer left, stay low, and strike anything in its path with horrible force.

Harry Weetman was a great slogger who in his time hit a lot of shots in that direction. I was playing with him in an exhibition match at Barton-on-Sea, in Hampshire. There was Harry on the tee, preparing to drive with one of his massive clubs (Harry's clubs were all about three inches longer than anyone else's and he brought them down with an awful crack).

I can see the spectator now, leaning forward for a better view. Harry was very conscious of his tendency to smash these low cutters, and he'd already waved back the people down the left-hand side. As ever, they'd crept forward again. This fellow was on the end. His left foot was forward, left hand on his knee, face turned intently towards Harry.

Harry's driver rose and he whacked the ball as if he'd club it to death. The ball rocketed off and caught the man just in the fleshy part at the back of the thigh. You've never heard such a scream of pain as came out of this man. He fell to the ground howling, his leg already swelling up like a balloon.

First aid came to him in the form of a rather sedate, spinsterish lady in a print dress and sandals. She went to work immediately, undoing the man's belt and, to the horror of the multitude (this was the Fifties), taking his trousers down and massaging the wounded part.

'Cover him up! Cover him up!' people were hissing as we arrived. For by now the blackened and throbbing upper leg was in full view and it was hard to tell where bruise ended and wedding tackle began. The poor man was carted off; another good spectator gone to the wall. Later we learned that the lady who had so adroitly debagged him was the matron at a local old folks' home, so knew what she was doing. How churlish of anyone to have doubted her motives!

Fore! and Aft!

Sometimes it's difficult for spectators to know where to stand at all, with any guarantee of safety. Even behind the tee. I once saw a fellow, a tremendous slogger, hit an air shot, then swing the club back in frustration and belt the ball out the back of the tee, where it whistled past the ear of some unready bystander.

And when you think of all those American Vice-Presidents knocking people over like ninepins, it's a wonder they have any spectators left in the States. In the heyday of Agnew, Ford, Johnson, you never knew where the ball was going. With Agnew, it might be a lob out to the right, for instance; not quite so hard if it hit you, but how could you know in advance whether you were going to be maimed or just have your hair parted? They ought to strike special medals for it: 'For Gallantry at the 4th tee, Oakmont, Pa, 1975 (or whenever), before the biggest hooker to hold high office.' That might be some consolation.

26

Rabbits and Hares

Rabbits have a lot of common sense. Perhaps it's because so many of them are brought up on golf courses (*there's* a subject for some bright young zoologist to study). When a rabbit scents danger, it freezes. That's something a lot of golf spectators would do well to imitate. Far too often, when they see the ball coming – out of the sky, clear as a bell, or even bouncing along the ground – they scatter. Start darting about like our other friend the hare when he's got a pack of beagles after him. In all the jostling, someone pushes someone over, another one trips over a hummock and sprains an ankle, and someone else runs straight into the ball. Clonk! If only people would stay still, and watch the ball, then at most all they'd have to do is duck, or turn sideways and let it go past, and they should come to no great harm.

      That's not to say that golf isn't a dangerous game. It can be, and players, particularly, shouldn't be deceived by the apparent gentleness of it. Players do, constantly, get hit by partners and opponents raising a club suddenly, and everyone who plays golf and wears spectacles really ought to invest in plastic glasses. Ordinary glass is just too risky. I've seen enough people badly hurt, even lose their eyesight, because they didn't take that simple precaution. However. End of sermon.

28

Reggie's Cowshot

My father told me once of an exhibition match he'd played at Westward Ho! with Reggie Whitcombe. The course was over common land and there were quite a few cattle about when Reggie hit a lowish one over to the right.

The ball arrowed towards a group of cows and embedded itself in the caked mud round the backside of one of these unfortunate beasts. Thwack! The cow reared up and clattered away in panic. It's difficult to know how much pain a cow feels at such moments, but Reggie's blow must have had a considerable impact. The cow wouldn't stop. The ball was a barely visible smudge, the lone silver decoration on top of a very animated chocolate sponge, as the cow heaved to the top of a ridge and galloped away to the seashore, perhaps in search of cooling waters. Watching it disappear, someone said to Reggie:

'That's the longest bloody shot you'll ever hit!'

As the cow continued its withdrawal, a lively debate broke out among the players. What to do next? Play a drop ball. Ah, but where? Where the cow collected. Ah, but that supposes the cow was an outside agency *in motion* when the ball lodged in her backside. The point is, the cow wasn't in motion *until* struck by the ball. That makes it an ordinary stop or deflection, which therefore counts as a rub of the green. Sorry old chap. Ah, but then Reggie has to play the ball *as it lies* . . . and the old cow hasn't stopped yet!

And on and on, until dusk fell. Little more is known of the cow. It's hardly surprising that she opted not to return the ball. Why, that Reggie Whitcombe might have got her again!

DROP!

PLOP!

The Clan Alliss

thought you might like to see my coat of arms. Here it is: As you will observe, it is divided into 3 parts by a pairle (Y shape). The top part (1st, arg.) is silver with a vinestock entwined with a grapevine, symbolic of France. The left part (2nd, sa.) is black with a cornflower plant with three natural flowers with green stems and leaves, symbolic of Germany. The right part (3rd, gu.) is red with a rose plant with three white flowers and green stems and leaves, symbolic of England. The upper left corner of the shield is purple with a gold grasshopper, symbolizing nobility. I wish you could see it in colour. For that matter, I wish *I* could see it in colour. This black-and-white version arrived one day from the United States, where genealogically-minded golf fans with surnames such as Alis, Allis, Alliss, Allice, Alys, Ellice or Ellis are forever sending messages over to the Old Country in their search for fresh ancestors.

Albert W. Allis of Cheektowaga, New York, tells me that nearly all the Allises in the USA are descendants of William Allis of Hatfield who in 1630 sailed from England on the third voyage of the *Mayflower*. And that a Richard Allis took the oath of allegiance in England in June 1632, embarked in the good ship *Lion* and arrived in Boston in September the same year.

(What has any of this got to do with golf? Get to the point, man. N.St.J.P.D.Q., Birkdale.)

I'm coming to that. But first you have to know that the earliest recorded

ALIS DRIVIUM VENIT hAROLD: SAC DRIVIUM

VVILLE!

IT'S YOUR LAST CHANCE WITH THE DRIVER, ALIS—THEN WE TRY THE SHOWER OF ARROWS...

Allises (I think it was my grandfather who added our extra 's') came over with William the Conqueror. William Alis, whose lands are listed in the Domesday Book, settled at Ellatune, now Allington, Hampshire, received a knighthood, went crusading and sat in Parliament.

Lately, I have been doing some of my own research into the early Allises. One day I was looking at some pictures of the Bayeux Tapestry, part of which shows the Norman army's boats arriving in the great invasion of 1066. I found myself examining a group of men-at-arms dressed in chainmail armour and bearing kite shields. One of them, instead of wielding the usual broadsword, held an altogether different, oddly familiar weapon. It had a long slender shaft and a head of wood and metal, flat on one side, curved on the other. I knew, instantly, that this must be William Alis.

Perhaps it was my fancy, but he did seem a trifle bewildered, all done up in chainmail armour and a conical helmet with a long noseguard sticking down the front, rather obscuring the view. What did he need all this for? Probably William had thought he was travelling to some Alliance meeting up the coast, and was quietly looking forward to nine holes before lunch, nine after and then a good feast with roast swan, partridge, boar, a few eels to start with, some of those eggs in jelly he liked so much, plenty of Gascon wine and sweetmeats ... wondering if they'd have a jester, like at the last place, who dashed into the room, jumped over their heads and straight into a huge bowl of custard – lasted three days, that one ... Dear old William. Imagine his surprise when Harold and the Pevensey team turned so aggressive. Still, he must have done all right, to survive and beget us all. Well played, William!

Quail High

n Texas they have a special term for the golf shot which keeps the ball fairly low so it doesn't get blown around in heavy wind. It's known as hitting the ball 'quail high' – at the flying height of a quail – and according to Ben Hogan it's a great deal more effective than being up in the clouds when the wind is blowing. The Texans also have a term for the ball that scarcely rises above the ground: that one goes 'mouse high'.

As a description, 'quail high' has a certain poetry that some of my more fiery correspondents would probably not wish to acknowledge in a phrase that was born in the United States. 'Whiff' is another Americanism I quite like – just as good as, and possibly more atmospheric than, the everyday 'air shot'. Americans, too, gave us the 'eagle', and they seem to be winning with their use of 'bogey', meaning one over par, as opposed to the original British use which referred to the score that a scratch player was expected to make; this has now been superseded, of course, by 'par'.

'Double-bogeying', meaning two over par, is less elegant, and provokes several acres of angry correspondence each year. 'Lagging up' for playing short is adequate, no more, but I am surprised by the antagonism it generates in the souls of some viewers.

'Trap' for 'bunker' is another perfectly innocent term that has them tearing up divots in the living-room carpet. 'Front-nine' and 'back nine' will be forever resisted in some corners of Old England. 'What's wrong with the "first half" and the "second half"?' they wail. 'Or simply "out" and "in"?'

Well, I'm not a grammarian, but I don't think you can have absolute rules about every expression. Most golfing terms have their variants, and it would be a dull language that never moved a little, accepting changes of usage when enough people want to see a change. And, like it or not, there *are* enough people in the USA; they've also been independent for some years – as I think we shall be hearing again in 1983. So perhaps a little more tolerance is called for on this side of the ocean.

Where I can sympathize is when Americans lapse into that awful pompous wordiness, using fifty-eight words instead of three or four. Scientists, computer people and the military seem to be chiefly responsible for these unfortunate developments – though here again we need to accept that the world is changing, has got more

complicated. So, to digress a little, if you're an Army general and you've got a highly sophisticated rocket that can do all sorts of things, you have to give it some kind of handle, preferably with initial letters that are easy to remember. Take MIRV, for instance. MIRV, I have found, stands for multiple independently-targetable re-entry vehicle; a bit of a mouthful, I agree, but if someone's built a rocket that can do all those things – warheads peeling off in different directions all the time – you can't very well ignore it, or call it 'Big Bertha' because you yearn for the old days. MIRV it's got to be.

On the other hand, there are times when Americans do get a bit tied up in mechanical jargon. Perhaps Douglas Bader ought to have the last word on this. He was once approached by an American who said, with great sincerity, how pleased he was to meet Bader, such a distinguished man, and so on. He then said there was something he was particularly concerned to know, and asked:

'What is the fatigue factor on your legs?'

Bader gave him an old-fashioned look and said: 'You mean, does it hurt? Yes, it bloody well does!'

THE FATIGUE FACTOR ON MY LEGS? — OH, I'D SAY ABOUT SEVEN DOUBLE SCOTCHES.....

The Off Day

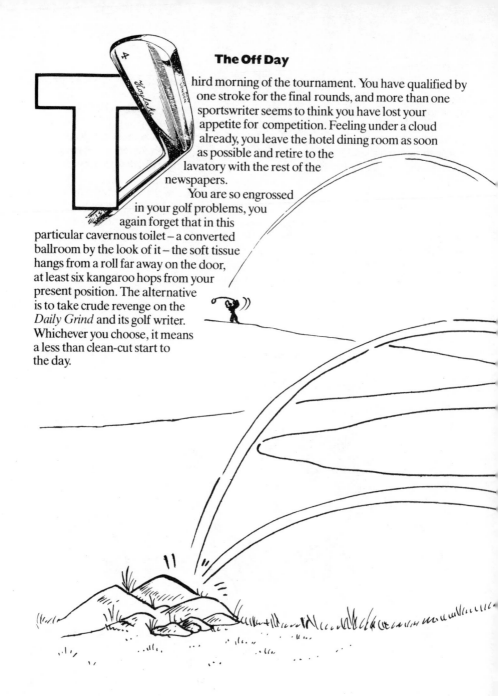

Third morning of the tournament. You have qualified by one stroke for the final rounds, and more than one sportswriter seems to think you have lost your appetite for competition. Feeling under a cloud already, you leave the hotel dining room as soon as possible and retire to the lavatory with the rest of the newspapers.

You are so engrossed in your golf problems, you again forget that in this particular cavernous toilet – a converted ballroom by the look of it – the soft tissue hangs from a roll far away on the door, at least six kangaroo hops from your present position. The alternative is to take crude revenge on the *Daily Grind* and its golf writer. Whichever you choose, it means a less than clean-cut start to the day.

Trouble strikes next in the car park. A shiny black TR-7 is in your space. *Your* space.

'Hey,' you call to the attendant. 'That's *my* space. I've been parking there all week.'

'Oh really, sir?'

'Yes. You ask your colleague, the ginger-haired fellow, he's been putting me in there every day.'

'I'm afraid I don't know anything about that, sir. And he's not here today.'

'Yes, but ...'

'Sorry, sir. Can't very well move the other gentleman now.'

Eyes half-closed in anger, you head for the locker-room. In your path you register a loitering figure you have recently come to loathe. Just the sight of his purple windcheater, his sallow unsmiling face sucking on his tenth King Size of the morning, makes you shudder. It's your fault, you should never have taken him on in the first place.

'Have you caddied before?' you asked him that first day.

'Oh, yes sir, yes.'

He then wrapped his great tobacco-stained banana fingers

round your bag as if tossing the caber, and you knew right away he had never picked up a golf bag in his life. Out on the course, he haunted you with his shadow – always looming across the line of your putt. Whenever you wanted the bag on the tee, he was always ten yards out of reach – looking the other way, like as not, at some female spectator ('Keep your grubby eyes off *my* female spectators,' you'd mutter to yourself, 'it's *me* they come to see.') You'd lift a club from the bag; 10 to 1 it would be covered with mud and grass. You would dearly like to ditch him, will do at the end of the week; but it's too late to change now.

'Good morning,' you say to him. 'All set, are we?'

'Orright,' he grunts, irritated that you have arrived halfway through his King Size and he must now stub it out.

Out on the course, with George as your partner. God! Why give me George? One of the biggest fairway lawyers in the game, always arguing the toss with his partner, caddy, referee, anyone he can get to listen to him. And slow! Jesus, if he gets round in under five hours he develops blisters.

From the start it is clear you are not on peak form. This makes you doubly nervous, anxious to get on to the next hole in the hope of erasing previous mistakes. George is his usual snail-like self. Cursing his misfortune at every missed putt.

'Oh Gaad! Why does it always happen to me? Anyone else hit that, it wouldda gone in.'

You know perfectly well that last one could never have gone in. It was always going to the right of the hole, with the slope, and short of defying the laws of gravity it was always going to miss. But you keep quiet. No point in provoking him.

Then at the next green George is preparing to putt. He stops, looks angrily round at you, and says:

'Will you ask your caddy to move? How can I play my shot if you let him stand there?'

The terrible thing is, the purple-pullovered oaf *is* standing with his shadow over the ball. So it looks as if old paranoid George does have a case, and *you've* set it up.

'Very sorry, George, can't think how he got there.' You seethe as the apology leaks out of your throat, and wave at your caddy who glowers back and shuffles grudgingly out of range.

The worst is yet to come. At the 12th, George hooks his drive well into the rough. You hit yours down the middle. There is a long pause. People are gathering. It's George. The referee is stumbling through the heather. George has decided that a television tower about 100 yards away was directly in line with his ball and the flag, and has moved his ball thirty yards to the left. A real argument is blossoming, and you, having hit your best drive of the day, and desperate to follow up, have no real option but to go over.

George is telling the referee that the television tower was obstructing him, that's why he moved his ball. It's in the rules. Interference in the line of play. The referee is telling George that he is suffering from severe delusions of grandeur if he seriously thinks he could ever have hit that tower from where he was. Besides, he should be playing back to the fairway, not up there. But George insists; the referee insists. Both men have a point. Meanwhile, your concentration is fractured ... and a plume of cigarette smoke is rising from the hand of a man in a purple windcheater standing next to the referee.

It's all more than you can bear. You three-putt at the 18th and finish with 83. Near the entrance to the clubhouse is the man from the *Daily Grind*.

'Never mind,' he says. 'Always another day.'

'Yes,' you say between clenched teeth. 'Bloody tomorrow!'

More Clubhouse Tales

he feudal code of the clubhouse, rest assured, is with us still. This little tale, which may or may not be true, is attributed to Brancaster Golf Club in Norfolk.

A visitor arrives to find a near-empty clubhouse, just the one old member in the corner behind a copy of the *Daily Telegraph*.

'Good morning, nice day,' says the visitor.

No reply from the old member.

'Hummm!' says the visitor bracingly, bouncing up and down on his heels.

'What a beautiful day! My first visit here. How glad I am to see the sun shining! It really is a quite delightful day.'

Still no reply from the old member.

'I've heard so much about this course. Can blow a lot, I know, but there's not a breath of wind today. It really is a marvellous day.'

The old member stirs, gets up and shuffles over to the bar. He presses the bell and soon the steward appears.

'Steward,' says the old member, 'would you look after this fellow. I do believe he wishes some conversation.'

Jewish Ups and Downs

The Jewish golf clubs are prospering as never before. This is because of the unprecedented number of Gentiles who are trying to become members. They have heard a rumour that you can get 10 per cent knocked off the gross before they deduct the handicap. Which is another reason, if you're Jewish, for staying at home and enjoying yourself. Who needs travel?

Two Jewish golfers, failing to heed this advice, went off on a golfing tour of Central and South America. The second country they came to, there was some minor irregularity at Customs, and by evening our friends were in front of the firing squad.

They were tied to stout poles, about ten yards apart, when the captain of the guard came up to the first one and asked if he had any last requests.

'No.'

The captain went over to the second unfortunate golfer and asked him if he had any last requests. In reply the golfer lifted up his head proudly and spat in the captain's face,

'I spit on you,' he said.

The first golfer turned on him and hissed:

'Hymie, for pity's sake. Don't make trouble!'

40

True Confessions

A Catholic golfer had only been playing the game for about three years. He was still very bad, just managed to scrape a handicap of 24, then suddenly he went out one day and played the game of his life; broke 80. He'd been on his own but hadn't cheated once, and had gone round in 54 net, off 24. Quite staggered by it all, he didn't know what to do. He left the golf club in a state of high excitement, went to his local church and entered the confessional.

'Yes, my son,' said the priest.

'Father, I went round in 78. Can you believe that? 54 net off 24. Can you ever believe it?'

He was so excited he got up and left without waiting for an answer. He went round the whole of the town, which was in a very strong Catholic region, going into confessionals and telling his story – 'Father, father, round in 78, net 54 off 24, how can it be true? I did it, I did it, can you believe me?' – and dashing off again to the next place.

Eventually, one elderly priest listened to him going on about his great feat, then said:

'My son, why are you telling me all this? You are not even of my parish.'

The fellow replied: 'Father, I'm telling everybody.'

The Pacemaker

I heard some good news from Alex Chilcott about one of his fellow-members at Croham Hurst Golf Club, near Croydon, where Alex is a past captain. The fellow had been pretty ill with heart trouble but then had had a Pacemaker fitted. This did wonders for him; he felt great and became pretty lively again. His home life, sex life, even his golf got better.

One weekday this fellow turned up at the club and found a visitor looking for a game. So they went over to the 1st tee together, and as they got there the member couldn't resist telling his story.

'I've got a Pacemaker,' he announced, with enormous pride in his voice.

The visitor replied: 'I'm playing a 65, number 7.'

Away The Rams!

Alex also told me that he belongs to a small golf society called The Rams. Once, at an away match, Alex had stayed in the bar because he was unable to play. While the others were out on the course, a member of the home club asked Alex who he was and what he was doing.

Alex replied that he and his friends were from Croham Hurst, they belonged to a small society called the Rams and they travelled around enjoying days out, good fellowship, wine and food. The member asked:

'What exactly does it mean – Rams?'

'Well, exactly what it implies,' answered Alex.

The member went white. 'My God,' he said, 'my wife is out on the course!'

Gone Fishing

Tommy Horton, a past captain of the PGA and a very successful golf professional at Royal Jersey, told me a rather good Henrik story. Henrik Lund is one of those people around whom stories accumulate. A qualified lawyer, Henrik is also a mad-keen golfer and used to turn up at tournaments all over the world. No-one knows how he managed it, but he did.

He is also a delightful eccentric, quite likely to turn up in Nigeria with the temperature at 100 degrees and 100 per cent humidity wearing four roll-neck cashmere sweaters and a Bud Flanagan overcoat and pretend that it isn't hot.

One year, the Italian championship was held at Pevero on the Costa Smerelda, part of the Aga Khan's very posh development on the north-east coast of Sardinia. Pevero is a wonderful course, but very hard, landscaped through rock with great boulders everywhere; go off line and you've had it. Anyway Henrik was there, and very early one morning he was first out for a threeball with David Russell and Tony Charnley.

It was bitterly cold, but they made the best of it and were nearly halfway round when they came to a long-short hole with water down the left-hand side. Russell and Charnley hit their balls onto the green, but Henrik knocked his into the water. It was still cold, a miserable day for April in that part of the world, the sun nowhere in sight, light rain falling.

They got up to the pond and Henrik did the customary thing, dropped a ball behind the hazard and chipped on. Just as they were moving past, Henrik looked down at the water and cried:

'There's my ball! Wait a minute, I'll just get it.'

He couldn't quite reach it from the bank with his club, so he took off one shoe and sock and rolled up his trouser leg. He stepped into the icy water, and reached out with his club but still couldn't quite get to the ball. Very deceptive, trying to reach things in water. So off came the other shoe and sock; the other trouser leg was rolled up to the knee. In he went again, waving and snatching with his clubhead, but he couldn't shift the ball.

Henrik pushed his trouser bottoms up as far as they would go, and had another try. Still the ball wouldn't move.

'To hell with it,' said Henrik. He took a deep breath, pinched his nose between two fingers, ducked his head under the water, opened his eyes and stared around. It was a bit dark beneath the surface, as well as freezing cold, but he at last located the ball, got hold of it and waded over to the bank. He climbed out, dripping from head to foot, all visible parts of him turning blue with cold. He glanced down at the white object in his hand, and his eyes narrowed; it was a golf ball all right, but it wasn't his!

Golf in the Head

Mad Mac, for many years Max Faulkner's caddie, had another client who looked after him very well. A quiet man, a bit of a recluse, he liked his round of golf, but preferred to play with imaginary clubs – which Mad Mac of course carried for him.

The fellow would go through the motions, with Mac supplying the sound effects, the swishing of the club, the crack as it hit the ball. Then Mac would cry:

'Oh, lovely shot, sir. Two hundred and twenty yards, just down the middle of the fairway.'

Then Mac hoisted the imaginary bag onto his shoulder, and they'd walk down the fairway. Mac handed his client a 7-iron, and watched him make his stroke.

'Whaackkk. Oh, well done, sir.'

One day they were going round, and had got to the 11th when the people behind them caught up. They were fascinated by what they'd been seeing. One of them asked Mac what on earth was going on, imaginary clubs, swiping at thin air and so on.

'Sshh,' said Mac, a finger to his lips. 'Don't you disturb him. He's four under par and that's the best he's ever done on this course.'

'What do you mean?' cried the fellow. 'It's crazy. You've got no clubs, no ball, what's it all for?'

'I'm not sure myself,' said Mac. 'Not a word to him, though. He hasn't got a car either, but he gives me a tenner a week to keep it clean.'

THE CADDIE MUST BE CRACKERS - *THAT* SHOULD HAVE BEEN *A NUMBER FIVE* IRON....

The Ideal Weekend

Not so long ago I was on a British Airways flight from Melbourne to London. The flight was smooth all the way, the service a delight in all but one aspect. As we hummed steadily above the deep-blue ocean, I did have time to ponder why, on that particular route where so many tongues are heard, the powers-that-be chose to put on two films that really in my humble opinion failed to fit the bill of general entertainment.

The first was called *The Earthling* and starred the late William Holden. I am a Holden fan but this macabre story of a dying man trekking miles into the backwoods to find the valley where he was brought up, coming across this boy who had been orphaned during a holiday with his mother and father in a motor accident and was wandering alone in the wilds, was really rather heavy stuff for 36,000 feet. During the film I looked round the cabin, at the faces of yellow and brown chattering amongst themselves, at the black domes of the Middle Eastern contingent, silent behind their yashmaks, and wondered if the moguls of Hollywood had not finally met their match.

The other film was very Glaswegian, and I'm told won lots of medals and awards at film festivals around the world. It was called *Gregory's Girl*, and told of young love in the 15 to 16-year-old bracket, and of a school football team into which the girl forced herself. Not perhaps the ideal subjects or even the ideal accents to try to decipher above the hum of those four mighty engines and the occasional Bangladeshi cackle. So I pulled out the plugs, ordered a glass of invigorating claret, and ruminated.

I had just been watching some golf in Australia and interviewing Peter Thomson, an interesting man if ever there was one. I got to thinking about golf, the places I have visited and the number of people who have asked me which was my favourite golf course. Yes, where *would* I go for my ideal round of golf? Who would be my ideal companions? There are so many golf courses, famous and not-so-famous, beautiful and ugly, that I have not yet had a chance to visit. So I was rather stuck with the ones I knew – and as I remembered them – but that left a fair selection. Hmmmm, I thought, as I put the seat back a notch and ordered another creative glass of claret, where should I start? I've got to start somewhere, so why not where I really learnt my golf, at Father's old club, Ferndown in Dorset.

Ferndown and Points West

When you look back on your youth, or your National Service days, after enough years have passed you only remember the good bits. And Ferndown gave me plenty of good bits to remember. Looking out of the window of my father's shop across the green acres that were always kept in beautiful condition, watching so many people come and go, seeing the till-roll being added up at the end of the day – none of those electronic monsters like now, just a paper roll with a couple of golf-ball boxes by the side to take the 'dibby' money. How marvellous it would be to recreate a game with some of my earliest friends from those early post-war days, many of them, alas, now departed: Joe Close, Harold Wakefield, Major Ruttle, Ralph Langton, Ted Chubb....

Not far away is my beloved Parkstone. That area round Bournemouth is blessed with marvellous heather, pine and gorse, and golf courses that dry out quickly and keep themselves in good condition. From 1957 until 1970 I was professional at Parkstone, starting off with my brother Alex who now lives in Guernsey. We had some wonderful years. Parkstone was more cosmopolitan than Ferndown and had a road going through the middle of it, quite a busy road for not far away was the little village of Lilliput where Dean Swift created *Gulliver's Travels*. To the south lay Poole Harbour. The views from the 8th tee were quite spectacular. In the small, cosy, unsophisticated clubhouse I would meet the secretary, J.D. (Daddy) Bond, with his delightful, slightly scatterbrained Scandinavian wife, and many friends including Brian Crutcher, the old speedway rider of Wembley, Southampton and England. Oh, yes, the time spent wandering around there, playing for a modest pound, coming in at the end of a winter's fourball, just as it was getting dark at about five o'clock, having a pot of tea, a few rounds of sandwiches, brown bread of course, with the crusts left on, and then someone suggesting:

'Damn it, it's a bit chilly, let's have a warming drink.'

If anyone said Whisky Mac, that was usually the start of a disastrous evening which might go on until about seven; then it was a case of leaving the car in the carpark and calling for radio cabs. Ah, but the brilliant conversation that flowed to and fro, the carefree happy banter. Days to remember.

Golf courses abounded in that area. There was the Broadstone, or Dorset Golf Club, to give it its more regal title. Arguably one of the most difficult pars in the country, a 68 with so many fine par fours of well over 400 yards. The walk down from the clubhouse over the old railway bridge, in the days when the trains stopped at almost every hamlet; back up the slope, over the bridge and into the clubhouse. Winston Churchill used to go and play there. I'm sure that old bath they had there was the one the old boy used to wallow in. The bars never closed, and the boiled eggs and toast for tea were an absolute delight.

Swanage and Studland, the Isle of Purbeck, and the great adventure of going across on the ferry from the Haven Hotel was really something to remember. The golf course in those far-off days was owned by Enid Blyton, of Noddy fame. The views on a fine day, looking back from Swanage and Studland, from the big windows of the Isle of Purbeck clubhouse, down across the heather to the inner reaches of Poole Harbour, across to the finger which stretches out and is called Sandbanks, with Bournemouth on the right and Poole on the left, will stay in my memory for ever.

Meyrick and Queens Park Golf Clubs, which I remember so fondly. Ernest Whitcombe of the great Whitcombes was the professional at Meyrick for so many years. As a lad of 16 and 17 I used to go and play there and find the old boy in winter in the back shop with the front of the stove open, toasting pikelets, bits of toast and tea

cakes, making mugs of tea; the smell of a gluepot boiling on a gas ring, old grips and hickory clubs. The number of old hickory clubs that must have had the head sawn off to be used as peasticks, or plugs for steel-shafted clubs – when you wanted to lengthen one, you just stuck a bit of hickory in the end and away you went. I wonder how many tens of thousands of poundsworth of golf clubs went that way.

Barton-on-Sea, which runs along the clifftop just to the east of Bournemouth, was also great fun but not to be tackled in a Force 9 gale. Andrew Jolly used to be the pro there. How well I remember his lovely ruddy face and his wavy white hair. He did enjoy a gin and tonic or two.

Highcliffe – a funny little course, almost the smallest 18 holes I know, on something like 50 or 60 acres, but every hole a good one. You always had to come in from the right angle; not much chance of a chip and a putt. The only trouble was that if anyone shouted 'Fore!' everyone else on the course hurled themselves to the ground.

The old Northbourne Golf Club, now Knighton Heath. It had Bill Knott's Bluebird caravan business on one side and Max Factor's factory on the other; not too romantic, it was rather looked upon as the working man's club, but what good holes abounded there. I always enjoyed my Alliance meetings at Northbourne.

Brockenhurst – not all that far away and up on the edge of the New Forest. Narrow and very appealing, it was also a favourite. But there are so many courses to remember and so many courses to see. How about travelling westwards.

Budleigh Salterton I remember. Belinda Lee, that lovely film star who was sadly killed in a car crash so many years ago – her father used to have the Rose Mullion Hotel which sat high above the course. Ah, the golf there with Arthur Robins the pro, and sneaking looks at Belinda when she was home from filming one of her epics...

... Indian Ocean still below. Still not a murmur from behind the yashmaks, despite steamy goings-on in the Scottish epic up there on the screen. Another claret? Perhaps not. Must push on, down through Cornwall.

49

Trevose. Owned by that little Cornish pixie Peter Gammon, son of Old Man Gammon whose name is still mighty in the Far Eastern construction industry. A day's golf at Trevose could be quite tempting: with Roy Connium, the professional; my son Gary, who was the assistant there when he was doing his apprenticeship and learning the trade, and perhaps Stanley, the waspish steward who's been there almost since the world began. What a fourball that would be.

TREVOSE

3 HOURS IS TOO LONG FOR A GAME OF GOLF !

If you have never been to Trevose, try it. Look from the clubhouse down the first fairway, but do not ignore the notices on the first tee. Such things as: 'Three hours is too long for a round of golf. Get on with it.' The binoculars perched in Mr Gammon's office, which scanned the course from time to time to see that no-one was diverted from their twoball or foursome into a fourball. If they did, and adopted the wrong attitude when remonstrated with by the young master, they risked being ordered off the course with their green fee handed back to them. When you get down by the 4th green you are very close to Booby's Bay, which has taken on an entirely new and interesting meaning since topless bathing has become all the rage. Back into the clubhouse, Gammon at the bar ordering a jar of buck's fizz, which gradually becomes the real thing, which gradually becomes brandies, which gradually becomes an afternoon's siesta.

Past St Enodoc to Westward Ho! How about that? Stan Taggart was the professional there for umpteen years. What about raking out old J.H. Taylor and Stan

Taggart? Who else might we get in? Perhaps Arnaud Massy might be over – the only Frenchman to win the Open. A fine swashbuckling character, and one-time private professional to the Pasha of Marrakesh, he would bring some spice to a West Country occasion.

Swinging along, we come to Minehead. I've only played there twice. I was stationed in the RAF Regiment at Watchet, about ten miles away, when I first joined their ack-ack gunnery school at Christmas 1949. The CO was a mad-keen golfer. He only lasted three weeks, though, and then one of those rugby-playing louts came in and my mid-week golfing activities had to be put on one side. But twice a month I did go to my brother Alex, who was then the professional at the Weston-super-Mare Golf Club which wasn't too far away and a delight to play at. Donald Hoodright, Jack Poole, George Irlam were all great golfing characters there. Perhaps a day there and gin and tonics and a Steak Diane at the old Atlantic Hotel would go down a treat.

Wales and the North

To Royal Porthcawl, where my father started his professional career just after the Great War. I remember going there first in the early Fifties. The Bournemouth Alliance used to play the South Wales Alliance, and this meant a hair-raising journey from Bournemouth to Porthcawl with Ernest Millward, who won the English Amateur Championship in 1952, driving his Alvis Speed 25 like a budding Fangio, buzzing round the little harbour in Porthcawl, past the Esplanade Hotel and the Seabank, up that long drive, past the great Miners' Home on the right-hand side which sat like some Heathcliffe monument looking out to sea, and then into the carpark. The corrugated iron clubhouse, battered by many a gale, but what a warm welcome inside. The big coke stove, the slievers of tea, long glass cups with the handles on, all the old magazines, the smell of history. The 1st hole has now been done in one, conquered by the young assistant pro. Well done, young sir! That may not be equalled for many a long day.

Pushing up through mid-Wales, tiptoeing along the border with England, we come to Whitchurch and the Whitchurch Golf & Country Club. How about stopping off there with those two adventurous lads, Leslie Welsh and Albert Minshall. Perhaps David Thomas would join us for a fourball. No, they're a bit dangerous, Albert and Les, wouldn't escape from there without a bit of a hangover; better tiptoe past.

51

North Wales and Llandudno. Ah, what fond memories and great chums abound in those parts. It was 1957, the first week in April, the PGA Championship and my first event registering from the Parkstone Golf Club. Up I went, which was an adventure in itself in those days, from Bournemouth to Llandudno, in a new bright red Vauxhall. I arrived, I saw, I conquered. Tom Jones was the pro in those days, one of the great characters of British golf. A staunch Welshman with a lovely tenor voice, Tom liked nothing better when celebrating than to get up and warble away. Nice to get old Tom out again.

THERE'S LOVELY...

On we go to Hoylake. Memories of 1949. Joining the RAF and playing a round with Guy Wolstenholme. He swears I went round the course from the back tees in army boots with borrowed clubs in 67. He usually gets things right; pity I can't remember, it must have been a hell of a round. Hoylake, one of the great traditional clubhouses, with huge windows looking onto the first fairway. The practice ground is in the middle, to get you ready for the frightening 1st hole, and the deadly finish. The hole over the orchard. That short hole with the out-of-bounds just two or three yards off to the left. What a frightener that was. Bit too difficult for me; I think we'll leave Hoylake alone.

On to Southport where my father played in one of the early Ryder Cup matches. Another look at Gumleys, the horrendous bunker which looks to be half the height of the Empire State Building. The old clubhouse perched up on high ground overlooking the course; again an opening par three for a short hole, rather like Lytham – nothing wrong with that if the hole's good enough.

Follow the railway line and you come to Hillside, much overshadowed by its grand neighbour Royal Birkdale, but what a fine test of golf. Perhaps the finish could be improved a little, but it's been there too long to think about change. A game there? Or shall we slip over to Royal Birkdale? My first look at Royal Birkdale was in 1954 when I had a really good chance of winning the Open Championship. The first that Peter Thompson ever won. I finished four shots behind him and didn't really use my brains to great effect, or my putter. Another of those clubhouses which stands on the 18th green. Sit upstairs and have a sandwich and a drink and look over the course and remember Opens, Ryder Cups and days gone by.

Round the corner and up towards St Annes. One of my favourite courses, St Annes. Everything is cosy there. I suppose it shows I'm just a country lad at heart. The clubhouse is only some fifteen or twenty yards from the little road which runs alongside. The entrance hall, the swing doors, the wide staircase; pictures of past captains, the panelling, the great room upstairs overlooking the 18th green, the dining room, the old lockers. The pro shop close at hand, the putting green, the trains chugging their way up the right-hand side of the course, as you went out, and the bungalows, the houses and the roads creeping in on the right-hand side coming home. Not a slicer's course, but one I always enjoy. How about going there? *Could be*.

Up into the Lake District. I have never played any golf there but one of my early mentors, Harold Wakefield, used to tell me that Windermere was a great delight – must do that before I get too old.

Over the Border

SCOTLAND

BEWARE
GOLF COURSES
EVERY
100 YARDS

And so to Scotland. And Turnberry. Now Turnberry I think of as one of the great golfing places in the world. With not too much cash and some imagination it could be turned into an absolute marvel. Turnberry sees the start of a run of tremendous golf courses up to Ayr and beyond. Troon – Royal Troon today – where I had one of the great days of my life some twenty years ago doing the prototype for what is now the Gary Player Golf Strip. Bob Ferrier, the entrepreneur and writer, Iain Reed the photographer and I were the only people on the course. It was late April, early

54

May, warm, almost too warm for one sweater. We went round the course, which was in immaculate condition, and the idea was formulated. I played well, but the powers-that-be decided that I wasn't quite famous enough for an idea that could last a year or two and make a few bob, and which has in fact lasted twenty years and made several bobs. At the last count it was rumoured that it appeared in several hundred newspapers every week, and if you think of a fiver or a tenner a go from each paper – not a bad little income. Missed out again, Alliss! Never mind.

Up to Barassie. Western Gailes, Glasgow Gailes. Courses that are well worth a visit. Slip into Glasgow, play at Killermont, that delightful little tree-lined golf course nestling almost in the middle of the city. Remembering Harry Weetman, one of the great sloggers, winning the Penfold Tournament there many years ago; either driving every green or playing safe with 5-irons. Harry of the sledgehammer blows, the tree-trunk legs and the delicate putting touch; sadly, no longer with us.

Across to Edinburgh – what a wealth of golf courses. Can't slip by without another visit to Bruntsfield, where I played The Boys' Championship in 1946. On to Dalmahoy, always a treat, now of course the venue of many great tournaments – and why not? It's ideally situated, plenty of room for car parks, and a fine finish for the telly: the 17th you can drive, the 18th almost, which makes ideal television. It was there, too, that I met my darling Jackey, in 1965, so it has very happy memories for me.

Outward we strike towards Gullane, and the great Muirfield itself – The Honourable Company of Edinburgh Golfers. Perhaps a night at the Greywalls Hotel, the chintzy chairs, the smell of burning logs, the view from the bedroom window up the 10th hole, the clubhouse, the marvellous food. No professional, of course; Jimmy Hulme, down the road at Gullane, takes care of everyone's needs. Muirfield in many people's eyes is the fairest, the greatest, the best seaside links course in the world.

Dunbar is not far away and North Berwick, steeped in history, and of course Musselburgh with its very ancient golf links – one of the first, if not *the* first, golf courses. Never played there. That really should be a pilgrimage. Up into Perthshire, and Gleneagles. A bit spoilt for choice here, though I think most people want to play the King's and the Queen's Courses. They have other courses at Gleneagles, but none has made quite the same impact. The hotel still goes on in all its majesty. Perhaps a game there with the entire Marchbank family: Ian, the long-serving professional, and his sons Brian and Billy. If one of them drops out I'll get Derek Brown out of the shop. Yes, Derek Brown, the marvellous shopkeeper for the Marchbanks. Get him out – if he hasn't sloped off to Sotogrande.

Thoughts stray to the delights of Pitlochry, which I haven't seen. Never been up to Nairn. Must go to Dornoch one day. Damn it, young Ben Crenshaw and his American mob have beaten me to it. Aberdeen has some fine courses, and there are some fabled friends up there.

Back down to Dundee and Carnoustie, arguably the most difficult links course in the world when the wind blows, and then to Rosemount and its two fine courses set in heather, pine and silver birch – my delight.

Newcastle to Southampton

England again, and Newcastle. How about a little trip out to Morpeth, or the Newcastle Golf Club, or Gosforth Park where you can combine a day's racing with some golf and a night at the Gosforth Park Hotel which is indeed very splendid. Onward into Yorkshire, to Moor Allerton, my old club, and Moortown, the scene of many tournaments and early Ryder Cups. The Harrogate golf clubs, always fun to play. Pannal, Oakdale, Starbeck – and of course Alwoodley. Now *there's* one to stir the soul, a real golf club. Full of doctors, lawyers, accountants and the like. I don't think any 'rough chap' has ever stepped over its portals, but it never gives you that impression. An old wooden verandah, a large putting green; Ian Duncan, son of the great George, has been the pro there for many years; at Alwoodley, too, you will find pine, heather and silver birch, and a course in immaculate condition, never seemingly crowded, one of the great places to play golf. A golf club, not a gin palace; sometimes it's criticized for that, though goodness knows why. I think it's marvellous. It might be the one – let's wait and see.

A little bit further south we come to Lindrick. Lovely Lindrick, home of the 1957 Ryder Cup matches, and the Sir Stuart Goodwin Foursomes. What a great man for golf was Sir Stuart. He underwrote the Ryder Cup, which we won, and then the foursomes. Lindrick, where John Jacobs's mother, Vivienne, used to be the stewardess. The delights of staying there, those morning breakfasts – platters of bacon and eggs, mushrooms and kidneys, fried bread, tomato, baked beans, hot toast, buns, huge pots of tea, home-made marmalade. And of course Jack Jacobs, the professional – the Duke. What a marvellous life he had: his golf, his shooting, his fishing, his games of cards, his smoked salmon. Yes, the golf pro's life, if you are lucky, can be bettered by none. Lindrick, beautiful Lindrick; perhaps that could be it.

But onward, onward, like de la Mare's Three Jolly Farmers, past Sherwood Forest, past the Notts Golf Club at Hollingwell, both quite majestic. Anyone who has never done the long drive down from the top road to the little dell which houses the clubhouse of the Notts Golf Club has missed a rare treat. The first three holes in some

BIGGEST HANDICAP HERE IS THE BREAKFAST..

LINDRICK GOLF COURSE

people's opinion are a bit pokey: round the corner and back again in the triangle. I rather like them. I wonder why they haven't planted a few trees there just to break it up a little, but I think Hollingwell is a truly great course.

Over to Birmingham and Little Aston, where I won my first tournament in 1954: the Daks. Memories of Dai Rees, Max Faulkner, Ken Bousfield. Must remember to take a tie, though, otherwise you can't get into the clubhouse.

Leaving Birmingham, swing into Norfolk. King's Lynn, have a look at their new course; cut through some of the nicest golfing country I know. Up to Brancaster, Hunstanton, or Hunston as the locals like to call it; up to Sheringham – a delightful place, but not when that East Wind doth blow! South towards Ipswich: Woodbridge, the Ipswich Golf Club, Purdis Heath, which is also a fine golf club. Nip up to Woodhall Spa, with its huge bunkers; in many people's opinion the best inland course in Britain, along with Ganton, near Scarborough.

Slip down the M1 to Woburn. I always remember Henry Longhurst saying there was this little oasis of land, this little plateau where superb golf could be made. And lo and behold! the Marquis of Tavistock, in conjunction with Carreras Rothmans, has done just that: created 36 holes of delight, winding through the trees, and a superb clubhouse with as good a meal as he will find in the universe awaiting the hungry golfer.

Huntercombe – was it really bought by Lord Nuffield because they wouldn't let him join, thinking he was just a motor mechanic? I wonder. South Herts, the home of Harry Vardon and Dai Rees. North London Golf Course, a bit wet in winter, perhaps a bit dry in summer, but what a warm welcome. Perhaps a game there would do us all good.

Stoke Poges, a course I have often thought should have been London's finest north of the river. Stoke Poges which was used for the setting of Ian Fleming's *Goldfinger*. Every time I go there I expect to see Oddjob and Sean Connery marching to the first tee.

Wentworth, and its West and East Courses. Marvellously bitter-sweet memories for me of the 1953 Ryder Cup matches which slipped through our fingers, and Dunlop Tournaments that I won. Memories of Tom Haliburton, the old pro who died whilst out on the course. What a wonderful way to go for an old golfing retainer. Ah, if I could only go round there again – perhaps with Max Faulkner and Henry Cotton.

Swinley Forest, now there's a special little course. Sheer pleasure, very much like Alwoodley in Yorkshire, a real golf club which I have always enjoyed playing at. But there is such a pocket of golf clubs in that area . . . Woking, Worplesdon, West Hill, New Zealand, The Berkshire, arguably the nicest of them all. I like The Berkshire, I haven't been there for many years, but the feel of it on a summer's evening, striding down that fairway for a quick 18 holes, was something to treasure. People used to get round in two hours in those days; even Bobby Locke, notoriously slow, used to get round in three hours; sometimes he'd do it in 2 hours 50 minutes, and still be pilloried for his efforts. He must be smiling to himself today.

Out towards Royal St George's and that wonderful stretch of land from Broadstairs to Dover. The Royal Cinque Ports, Deal ... and St George's. I always remember Henry Longhurst saying that if he hadn't retired to The Windmills, his house high above Brighton, he would have gone to Sandwich. Asked why: well, he'd explain, there were always some interesting people at the club so there was always conversation, always interest, liveliness, and Mr Holley, the wonderful steward, and his wife kept a marvellous table – and 'the bar has been known to stay open'. There, too, the Whiting family, the only professionals at the club since it began; the wonderful old pro shop, full of golfing treasures. Oh, to sit out on the lawn at the back of the dining room and savour an early-evening Pimm's in the right company. Look across there, that's Stanford Tuck, the great war ace. Look over there, there's Gerald Micklem who's done such a lot for the development of golf. Who knows, Raymond Oppenheimer may appear. What a horn of plenty is St George's.

Round the corner to Brighton, past Sleaford, past Brighton & Hove and the Dyke, on to Pulborough, West Sussex, another splendid course. Liphook and Hindhead – Hindhead with its spectacular views and its nine or ten flat holes, and the other eight which help to keep the waistline down.

Farnham and Hankley Common, with greens that the great Bobby Locke always said were the finest in the land, and should never have overgreen mowers used on them; but of course they had to use them, and according to Locke the greens changed. But the setting and the course have not, and it is still a delightful place to play. Camberley Heath, and on to Southampton. Stoneham, a warm welcome to be assured there. North Hants. Ah, so many, and so many we have not had time to consider. Still, there's Ferndown on the horizon again, and our Round Britain tour completed. How about a quick flip across to the Continent?

Europe

The courses around Paris take a lot of beating. Elegant people. Men who never seem to wear overcoats, or certainly do not put their arms through the sleeves; some of them have got cigarette holders and coloured shoes – do you think they are all right? Shapely ladies, bumps in the right places. Smart clubhouses, the smell of parma ham and melon, mushroom omelettes and wine, fresh bread.

A visit to La Baule and the Hermitage Hotel, situated right on the best beach on the eastern Atlantic shore, a sort of European Copacabana. Ah, the food and the service. Five or six miles away the golf course, little shuttle service up there, thatched roof, cold beer, smoked ham rolls. Mmm, *that* could be it!

The South of France: Mandelieu, Montagel at Monte Carlo, Mougin near Cannes. On to Italy, to Olgiata and the Roma Golf Club. Even the Ancient Romans had a form of golf, or so it has been claimed. The Julius Caesar version was called *paganica*, which may sound like the sport of thrashing pagans, but probably wasn't, since the Romans were of that ilk themselves. No, the best sources have it that to play *paganica* you used a bent stick to hit a ball stuffed with feathers. I can't see it catching on. The Italians, though, have some wonderful golf courses. Milan, Turin, Varese. How about Lake Como. Como – there's a wondrous hotel for you. Look out from the rooms and see them water skiing and hang-gliding, towed behind a motorboat. It's not only the French who are loony, then!

Down to Spain. Sotogrande – my favourite – and along past the Porto Banus to Malaga; so many courses to choose from. What about a showbiz game down at Andalucia – Sykes, Connery, Tarbuck and me. If one of them can't turn up we'll get young James Hunt out; I expect he would bring that bloody Alsatian of his. Not a bad chap to have, though, Oscar – particularly in a dark alley in Malaga late at night.

The Algarve. Let's get Henry and Toots Cotton. They can use a buggy. We can play all those courses, ending up at Penina and having lunch, on Henry, in the Grill Room of course.

What about Scandinavia? All those courses around Stockholm. Trips up through the fjords, playing off mats, a strange mixture of wondrous courses and little knock-about places. Get Sven Tumba to fix me up with a game, as long as I've got Sven on my side; if we can't beat them Sven will talk them out of anything. Denmark, Holland. Ah, Holland. Some super courses there, The Hague in particular. Belgium. People do not often think of Belgium as being a golfing country but how well I remember being summoned by the then Prince Baudouin for some golf. Being picked up by himself alone in a 300-SL gull-winged Mercedes, the clubs in the back. Off to the Summer Palace here and the Summer Palace there, and golf courses which were quite superb.

Into Germany. Have a quick look at Berlin and Wannsee, where I was born. Not the same Wannsee my father opened in 1926. Some good courses in Germany – Düsseldorf, Cologne, Bremen. Playing through the forest, such a strikingly European atmosphere.

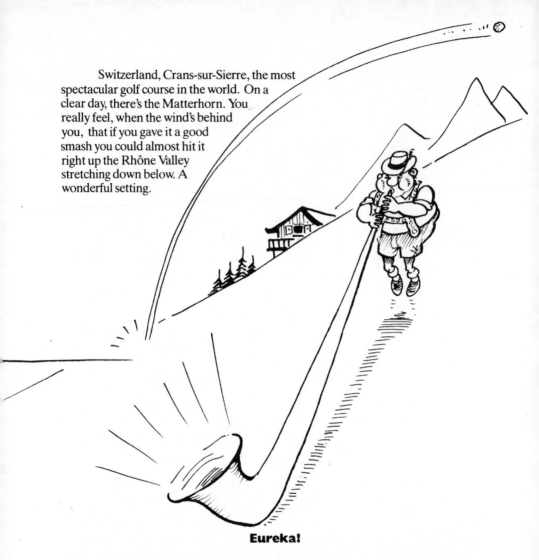

Switzerland, Crans-sur-Sierre, the most spectacular golf course in the world. On a clear day, there's the Matterhorn. You really feel, when the wind's behind you, that if you gave it a good smash you could almost hit it right up the Rhône Valley stretching down below. A wonderful setting.

Eureka!

What about America? So many places to see. Get on a plane to Cypress Point. On a plane . . . gem of a course . . . . As I woke from my reverie, the plane was still droning its way towards Muscat. And then it came to me! The ideal day, the ideal weekend, the fantasy to end all fantasies!

Where would it be? Well, on very close reflection it would be at the Sunningdale Golf Club. Why? Because I think Sunningdale has everything about it that a golf club should. The car park is handy, the pro shop has character, the caddie master's office has been smartened up over the years. You mount the steps to the entrance hall, the men's bar is on the right with the honours boards round the walls – such famous names; the bar is well-stocked and welcoming. The fireplace; a picture of Jimmy Sheridan, the old caddie master, hangs in the corner. Upstairs, the members' locker room and a little card room outside the Secretary's office. And there, looking down benignly, one of the greatest characters in golf, Arthur Lees, the professional for so many years. The dining room. The young chef carving those wonderful joints of meat. Pork, beef, lamb. Prawn cocktails, fresh melon, smoked mackerel, brussels sprouts, runner beans, broad beans, french beans, roast potatoes, mashed potatoes, thick dark brown hot gravy, apple pie, gooseberry tart, treacle tart, cheddar cheese, camembert, crunchy celery, club claret – oh! what a delight.

But who to play with? Why not go for the immortals? So, if I could manage two days, I think for my opening fourball I would like to step out with Walter Hagen (1892 – 1969), Joyce Wethered (1901 –   ) and Bobby Jones (1902 – 72). How splendid to find out whether Hagen was really an early version of Arnold Palmer, hitting balls everywhere and escaping with wonderful recoveries. Whether he was as smart and handsome as the brief snatches of Movietone News would have us believe; whether he was really as articulate as he seemed. Style had a lot to do with it, I suspect. And Bobby Jones. I would love to see his swing, his poise. Having only met him, sadly, in the autumn of his days, I could never otherwise see him thinking his way around Sunningdale, where his scorecard, which tots up to 66, hangs in the Mixed Lounge. And Joyce Wethered – well, such a wondrous player, now in her eighties, still bright and alert, interested and interesting. Yes, that would be quite an opening fourball.

The next day, having recovered from all the culinary delights of Sunningdale – and a halved match, I hasten to add – I can think of nothing better on the Sunday, after a leisurely breakfast, than playing with Harry Vardon (1870 – 1937), Babe Zaharias (1915 – 56) and Ben Hogan (1912 –   ). Why? Well, I've seen so many pictures of Vardon, listened to so many tales from my father, who incidentally, I'm sure, would have insisted on coming around and pushing my trolley, or even, if he was feeling quite lively, carrying a small bag. I have listened to so many tales of Vardon, and seen so many pictures which seem to contradict his great style, elegance and poise, I would just like to see the real man for myself. Babe Zaharias – what a difference between her and Joyce Wethered, Babe a real 'slugger' but surely one of the greatest athletes of our time. A splendid lady whom I only saw hit two golf balls. The same could be said of Ben Hogan: at Carnoustie in 1953, he was surrounded by thousands whilst I was battling my way around the course with ten – spectators, that is. So there it is, the Babe and I (ever gallant, you see, we Allisses) taking on Vardon and Hogan.

How about that for a little golfing fantasy.

Artificial Stimulants

don't know why they send them to me, but lately I've been receiving bizarre tracts and begging letters which all seem to have a common theme – the use of drugs, or mood-elevators, as I believe the shrinks call some of them, in our great game.

To take a sample begging letter, I was sent this from The Rescue Mission, Birmingham:

Dear Mr Alliss,
Perhaps you have heard of me and my nationwide campaign in the cause of temperance. Each year for the past fourteen, I have made a tour of Scotland and the North of England including Manchester, Leeds and Glasgow and have delivered a series of lectures on the evils of drinking. On this tour I have been accompanied by a young friend and assistant, David Powell. David, a young man of good family and excellent background is a pathetic example of life ruined by excessive indulgence in whisky and women.

David would appear with me at lectures and sit on the platform wheezing and staring at the audience through bleary, bloodshot eyes, sweating profusely, picking his nose, passing wind and making obscene gestures, while I would point out that he was an example of what drinking etc, can do to a person.

Last summer, unfortunately, David died. A mutual friend has given me your name and I wonder if you would care to take David's place on my next tour.
Yours in faith,
Rev Rupert R. Knight,
Rescue Mission.

Mint Freaks

Via a friend in Bournemouth, who reported that his regular golfing partner had begun putting like a demon after giving up smoking and living instead on Polo Mints, I received the following learned paper:

R & A Committee (Rules)
Fox House,
Glacier Street,
Bournemouth.

Subject: Investigation into the use of drugs as applied to mid-handicap, upper/lower quartile age group golfers to identify the organic, digestive, bowelic, inhibitive, additive, sexualistic effects thereof.

Sir,
My committee has instructed me to write to you re. the above – as it applies to yourself.

It has been brought to our attention that you are in the habit – during actual play – of eating/sucking/crunching a proprietary brand of mint (commercially sold as Polo).

Whilst this activity may, on the surface, appear to be quite innocuous, I have to bring to your attention the fact that, as the forementioned mint may contain up to 0.000183 mg/csl (by volumetric ratio) of the substance dihexythedrylanicmexain, it can, under certain conditions, viz before, during, after or instead of alcohol or sex – or in moments of high emotional stress, eg first tee on a Sunday morning, be considered to be a drug within the meaning of the act.

Although, legally speaking, the intake of such artificial aids does not contravene the R & A Rules, such actions are not considered to be in the best interests of the game.

Having read reports regarding your standard of play (quite amusing really) my Committee accepts that you are obviously in need of something to counter-act the depressive nature of your normal game. However, whilst we have no statutory powers to order you to stop taking this power-driving, one-putting aid we would urge you to:
a) Limit your in-take to the hours of bunker play.
b) Resist the temptation to whistle through the centre hole whilst your opponent is on his back-swing.
c) At least – hand the bloody things around.
I am, Sir
Your Obedient Servant

Ivor Trebor

Better After Lunch

I don't really know what to think, but for balance I feel we could do worse than quote this poem from A.C. Gordon Ross's collection, *A Mixed Bag of Golfing Verse*:

Of all the members in our set
At least there's one I won't forget –
I mean old Major Cuthbert Crunch
Whose game was better after lunch.
Three whiskies for aperitif
Afforded him but scant relief,
His lunch was of the liquid sort
He veered from vodka round to port.
The vodka never was much use
Till mixed with cold tomato juice –
Then oatcakes and some stilton cheese
With one full glass of sherry, please!
Then he had coffee laced with rum
Before being fit for all who come

But stop! Fill up the brandy flask
To carry which, his caddy's task.
A port and lemon capped the lot
This final touch I near forgot . . .
Thus fortified, the Major went
Out of the club-house, well content
To meet his cronies on the tee
His average score was ninety-three . . .
The Major lived to seventy-seven,
And now I hope he's safe in heaven –
That cruel relenting fate still yields
Some golf on th'Elysian fields
Post-prandial, with ambrosia strong,
To help the old chap's game along.

Proper Gear

or the many who receive their golfing baptism on a municipal course, the rules and social etiquette can seem mystifying at first. Even the essential weapons of the game are something of an unknown quantity, though people are usually quick to learn, and after a few holes you will hear their confident shouts:

'Ere, John, bung us one of them little flat ones.'

John, if he has his wits about him, will select a putter from the shared bag, whirl it twice round his head and send it winging over to his partner at the back of the green.

'Oops, sorry mate,' he may say if the club digs in short and his partner is spattered with mud and grass.

Another novice who hadn't quite spotted the full potential of his armoury when he set out on his round, got quite upset. It was down at Meyrick Park, Bournemouth, and he stormed back to the pro shop to confront John Stirling.

'Yes, sir?' said John.

'This place, it's a bloody swindle!' he raged.

'Oh, and why's that, sir?' asked John.

'These clubs. You charged me three pounds to hire these clubs.'

'Yes. Is anything the matter with them, sir?'

'Matter? For God's sake man, just look! They're not even all the same length!'

Trousers in the Socks

A scandal broke out the day Raymond Floyd decided to combat the wind and the wet by tucking his trousers in his socks. The trouble was, he was televised in the act. The repercussions were even worse than if the Club Secretary had been caught *in flagrante* in the boiler room with the new barmaid.

'I would be interested to know if my eyes were playing tricks with me,' wrote one typical viewer, still evidently in shock. 'In my Golf Club (320 mem.) we are trying to raise the Standard of Members, and this practice is *not allowed* … The problem can be quite easily overcome by wearing over-trousers and, underneath, trousers in the socks in wet conditions.'

Quite so. Standards must be maintained, raised even. Use this Below-the-Waist guide to check how your latest outfit will be rated on the modern golf course.

In	Acceptable	If you leave now, your green fee will be refunded
Plus-fours	Over-trousers	Trousers in socks
Plus-twos worn by women	Bermuda shorts worn by American visitors	Plus-twos worn by men; Bermuda shorts worn by English visitors
Expensive slacks	Well-cut, pressed jeans with French label	Denim overalls
Clean golf shoes	Muddy golf shoes	Trainers
Green wellington-type winter boots	Black wellington-type winter boots	Waders

Norman The Debunker

I wonder if that standard-raising viewer had ever seen Norman von Nida in action. Norman was one of the grittiest professionals on the post-war circuit, an Australian who steadfastly refused to let the laws of 'good form' run his life if he thought he had a better idea.

One bitterly cold April day at Southport & Ainsdale, Norman put his head out of the clubhouse and instantly knew what he must do. He fetched his overcoat, a great camel-haired double-breasted creation that swished about his ankles (Norman was only about five feet six), wrapped himself in it and stepped off to the 1st tee. To begin with, Norman took off the coat to play his shots, then got back into it. Unfortunately, it wasn't his day. By the 9th hole his score was in the region of 46, and he decided on a change of tactics: he'd keep the coat on all the time.

For those who saw them, the next nine holes were a rare treat with Norman, pugnacious and cursing beneath the black onion-seller beret he always wore, thrashing and smashing his way round the course, the giant overcoat whizzing round as he followed through. That day he buried the notion that novices had a monopoly in eccentric golfing attire.

Norman was definitely his own man. He demolished a bunker once. *He* thought he was doing the club an enormous favour at the time. There he was in this deep bunker which had an overhang in the direction he wanted to go. After his ball had struck the underside of the overhang two or three times and trickled back, Norman got the measure of things and dug himself out.

He wasn't happy, though, about this overhang. There was something wrong in having a great hunk of turf protruding over the edge of the bunker. He took his club and methodically began to chop out the overhang, carrying the pieces away and hurling them into the bushes. Meanwhile the press were happily snapping away at this odd spectacle of von Nida redesigning a bunker in the middle of a tournament.

Confronted later by the then Secretary of the PGA, the splendid Commander Charles Roe, RN retd, Norman was staggered that anyone should have taken offence.

'It was unfair,' he protested. 'I was just tidying it up for them.'

When is a Hole in One?

Anyone who has ever felt uncomfortable because, in the beginning, he or she didn't quite understand what an eagle was, or a birdie, take heart. Others have gone through this.

For many years I played exhibition matches with Dai Rees and others for the Lord Roberts Workshops and Forces' Help Society. One of our stunts for raising cash was to ask the spectators to fork out for various feats we might achieve: sixpence for birdies, a shilling for an eagle, five bob for a two, and so on. Before we started Dai, always the ringleader, would get people to put their hands up and, as it were, place their bets. The biggest payout was for a hole in one – that was a tenner. The thinking behind this was that no-one ever got a hole in one, or hardly ever, so for the basically mean spectator who wanted to look big, it was a pretty safe bet; on the other hand, we could do quite well with the more generous punters by putting away the birdies and piling up the sixpences.

We were at the South Staffs GC, Wolverhampton. Dai did his spiel at the 1st tee, and we signed up a good batch of punters – including about eight who were staking the hole in one. So what happens, Alliss gets up on the 2nd tee, a short hole, 8-iron, bonk ... straight in the hole for one.

When it was time to collect, Dai was doing great business. We'd got a good pile of birdie money, another for the eagles, and half a dozen tenners for the hole in one. Then up came this thin, rather parsimonious-looking individual, and produced a fiver.

Dai said: 'What's this then? Come on, sir, you had your hand up for a tenner.'

'Ah,' said the man. 'I'm only paying half price. You said a hole in one. It bounced twice before it went in.'

Star Turns

he siege goes on. Not a week passes without some ardent purist, or so-called purist, assembling the verbal equivalent of a Molotov cocktail, inscribing my name on the outside, much as aircrew did in the war (ZIS VUN FOR YOU, PETER!) and plopping it into the letterbox, the scent of ultimate victory in his nostrils. I get to know the handwriting. I can even see them coming by the quirks of their typewriters. The message seldom varies: 'We don't want to hear the ramblings of comedians, trade unionists, actors, politicians, etc, chewing things and telling jokes in the worst possible taste. We want to see more golf. Give us more golf. If you don't give us more golf ... Grrr ... '

Trouble is, I think they've got their priorities in a bit of a twist. There's enough *proper* golf, surely. By that I mean the various professional tournaments culminating in the Open Championship. That's proper golf. *Pro-Celebrity Golf, Around with Alliss, Men v Women* – that's a joyous mixture of beautiful scenery, good golf, some bad golf, and conversation, which even the purists, especially the purists, ought to file under the mental heading 'Entertainment', as they scan next week's *Radio Times* or the morning paper to see what's in store.

Because conversation is such a staple element of a programme like *Around with Alliss*, I get given a lot of biographical material about the people I am to meet. Much of it goes unused, but I was fascinated again the other day to come across the brief for Douglas Bader, and the story of how, already minus both legs in a flying accident, he got the golf bug and fought to get on terms with it.

The Man with the Uphill Lie

It was in the Thirties. Pilot-Officer Bader, the daring flyer, once brilliant at rugby and cricket, was something of a broken idol. His terrible crash at Woodley Aerodrome, near Reading, had meant the amputation of his right leg above the knee and his left leg below the knee. At Roehampton Hospital they fitted him with metal legs, and he learnt to walk again, to drive a car, even to pilot a plane; but the RAF would not have him back in peacetime – though they were glad to see him in 1939, when he achieved his most astonishing exploits as a fighter pilot.

One day in the early Thirties, still wobbly on his new legs, he accepted a friend's offer of a 7-iron, and started to try and hit a golf ball. He fell over twelve times before he made contact. He tried a slower and less dramatic swing, and began to strike the ball – and stay on his feet. That was enough. Golf became an obsession. Practising at the North Hants Club, he brought his old sporting skills to bear, his fine co-ordination of eye and muscle, and his steely determination. He started to play several holes – three, six, nine, then got up to 18. He began to go round in under 100, his wife Thelma his ardent caddie and chief source of encouragement.

Bader's handicap was down to 18, and he was playing in competitions when word of his great deeds reached Henry Longhurst, then one of our most distinguished amateurs – he won the German Amateur Open in 1936. Longhurst came down to the North Hants and was most impressed when Bader went round in 81. They played many times, and Henry made quite a study of Bader's extraordinary game.

Already, Bader had persuaded Roehampton to attune his metal legs to golf by fitting a kind of universal joint at each ankle. This gave him the lateral freedom he needed to straddle his legs and place both feet flat on the ground, whereas previously his feet had been tipped uncomfortably against the inside of his shoes.

Now as they played, Henry began to notice that Bader struck the ball particularly well on his second shot at the 5th hole, where the fairway sloped gently up to the green. He thought it might be because the uphill lie made it easier for Bader to get squarely behind the ball, and also helped the resistance down his left side as he struck the ball and followed through. They discussed this, and agreed that it would be an ingenious move to take half an inch off one leg so that Bader could enjoy the same effect on level ground. 'Wish I could do the same,' Longhurst added.

Bader took the proposition to Roehampton, but they feared it would create a bend in his spine. Bader said he'd risk that, his golf mattered more. So the leg was trimmed, and to good effect. Bader felt better for it, and his golf seemed to benefit also. When Henry heard the news, he wrote a piece in the *Evening Standard* about the man who had removed half an inch from his left leg so that he could play golf with a permanent uphill lie.

When he saw the article, Bader rang Henry in a state of some excitement. 'You goat,' he said, 'I had it taken off the right leg, not the left one.'

'Good God,' said Henry, 'you've taken it off the wrong leg!'

My Partner

We try to maintain an atmosphere of sweetness and light at the Pro-Celeb, and it is rare indeed for one of the participants, whether pro or celeb, to pass a disparaging remark about the chap he's been playing with. It follows that Lee Trevino must have been thinking of some other course, some other occasion, when he described a former partner as being 'about as much use as an ashtray on a motor-bike'.

Frank Carson must have had a similar experience. A homely, if sometimes strident, Ulsterman, Frank declared: 'My partner is about as much use as a chocolate fireguard!'

Dracula's Lunch

It had not occurred to me when Christopher Lee entered the great dining room at Gleneagles that in real life the star of all those epics of supernatural behaviour would wish to make strange demands on the kitchen staff. But there he was, the Transylvanian aristocrat, The Dark Avenger, The Man Who Could Cheat Death, Rasputin The Mad Monk, I Monster – to borrow just four of his titles – advancing

through the dining room to join us at table. A quiet man, though, for all his blood-stained repertoire. Gaunt of face perhaps, but distinguished, about six feet three. And enormously successful; probably one of the most instantly recognizable faces in the world, from Brixton to Bombay and Buenos Aires, wherever Horror is big.

The cooks had laid on a marvellous cold buffet that day. Sweetmeats overflowed from the scooped-out backs of ice swans, four feet high; there was quail, turkey, beef, salmon, roughly five hundred different sorts of vegetables, with salads to match.

Christopher Lee sat down. He accepted a menu from one of the waiters, and scanned the pages of that great document, a clear rival in volume and authority to the Ten Commandments. (And rightly so. For was this not the hotel where, with my own eyes, I saw the head chef arriving one day in a *powered hang-glider* with the first grouse of the season. I didn't even know there were such things as power-driven hang-gliders until I saw this aerial lawn-mower dipping over the trees.)

THE GROUSE IS ON THE LEFT, M'LORD...

The menu at Gleneagles is indeed worth a course or two by itself, so the waiter gave Lee plenty of time, and when he appeared to have made his choice, advanced again.

'Would you like to give your order, sir?' said the waiter.

'Yes,' said Lee, in the suave voice that has struck terror and passion into the vitals of many a celluloid virgin. 'I think I'll have a dish of peas.'

'Peas, sir,' said the waiter, scribbling the order quickly enough on his pad and looking up for more.

'Yes,' said Lee. 'And a glass of water.'

So, while those around him debated whether to attack the grouse, or the pheasant, or some other of those succulent carcasses recumbent on the squadrons of silver trolleys drawn up against the walls, the King of Darkness sat spooning in his bowl of peas. A chastening day for any who might have thought that the Star was always the Man.

Tarbuck's Fizz

One of the Pro-Celeb regulars is Jimmy Tarbuck, and I am grateful to my old friend Gordon Dean for this story of a rather special day out with Jimmy at my old club Parkstone, in Dorset.

Young Tarbuck, ever keen, had persuaded Gordon to foresake the office desk for an hour or two, and Gordon had popped in first thing to tell the staff he would be out most of the day 'on a survey'. By 10.30 he and Tarbuck were out on the first tee. It was a sunny day, light breeze, bracing conditions, and they played briskly round to the 14th.

Tarbuck struck a firm tee shot, dead straight. He stepped back to admire the trajectory. On, on went the ball, still heading for the flag, bounced a couple of times … and plopped out of sight just where it was meant to. Had he been on-stage, the next few minutes would have been from a review entitled 'Tarbuck Jumped Over the Moon'. His first hole in one! Absolutely delighted, he could barely wait to get back to the clubhouse and out with the bubbly.

Not another soul was about, apart from the steward, when they finished their round, but they enjoyed their celebratory sandwich, and a glass or two, then Gordon headed back to his office and Tarbuck made for The Pavilion, where he was doing a Summer Season. At the office they always had an early edition of the *Echo* to scan the property pages. When Gordon arrived, a clipping from the stop-press announcements lay in the middle of his desk. It said: 'Jimmy Tarbuck playing at Parkstone golf club this morning with one of the members Gordon Dean, holed his tee shot at the 14th hole.' Underneath, Gordon's manager had written: 'Some Survey!!'

Gordon swears that Tarbuck swears he didn't tell the *Echo*, but 'there were only the two of us. Beware your sins will find you out!'

'blame it on the steel shaft. That and mass-production. Once they'd been accepted as facts of life, the next step was inevitable, wasn't it? Eh? What d'you mean, what happened? What happened?' The speaker looked as if he was going to levitate off his seat and crash into the luggage rack. 'I'll tell you what bloody happened!'

It was an evening some years back. I was travelling by train from London to Leeds in a compartment without a corridor. The only other occupant of this buffet-less padded cell was a man of about 43 with staring eyes, wearing an Oxbridge tie. Having no option but to listen to his rantings, I did so with as much good humour as I could muster.

'The blasted accountants moved in!' he roared. 'That's what happened. All these new golf factories were kitted out with adding machines and those swingweightometer things to see how heavy the clubs should be. Operated by a bunch of retrained laceworkers, so I'm told. Anyway, then the chief blokes on the factory side ganged up with the accountants, and they put together these tables to tell the average golfer how to choose his golf clubs. Bloody cheek! All scientifically worked out on graph paper, one table for each club. "Name: 1-iron. Length: 40 inches or 1016 millimetres. Angle of loft: 17 degrees. Distance: 215 yards or 197 metres." And so on. Yards of the stuff, streaming off the machines like bog-paper. They'd even got what they called a profile of the average club player. "Male. Age 43. White. Father of two unruly teenagers. Suffers from dyspepsia. Strongly developed taste for wife evasion. 12 handicap." What tosh!

YOUR ACCOUNTANTS RECOMMEND A NUMBER EIGHT IRON, SIR....

'Next thing, while the managing director was across the road in the Frog and Nightgown drinking glasses of gin and tonic water, nicely topped up with cubes of ice and large slices of lemon, a fresh one with each round, the chief accountant and the foreman of swingweightometer operatives took over his office. They called in the Mashie, the Mashie-niblick and the Niblick, and said, in so many words: "On your bikes".

'After all those years of service, and not so much as a gold watch or even a thank-you. Disgusting! Two days later they were replaced by a grey-looking bunch of teetotallers who answered to numbers. Not an individual name between them. There was 5-iron, 7-iron and 8-iron. Then the management johnnies got to work on the blaster. Turned him into a sand wedge! I ask you! Making ciphers of us all.'

At this point the speaker seemed suddenly to run out of venom. He slid sideways in his corner seat and began to snore; leaving me to decide whether I had unluckily turned over a stone and come face to face with the King of Toads, or whether there had been a grain of sanity in the fellow's outpourings.

Obviously, he was a romantic of the more demented sort. But perhaps he did have a point. Perhaps some of the old charm has been lost since the days when no two clubs were ever quite the same. My thoughts went back to Scotland, one hundred years ago, to the age of the guttie ball and the hickory shaft . . . .

Sole Mates

Writing in the 1880s, Sir W.G. (Walter) Simpson, Bart, had plenty to say about clubs and their individual quirks. You may even think he goes too far at times, but there – you can't please all the customers all the time. According to Sir W.G:

'Nearly everyone carries a play club [driver], an instrument consisting of many parts. It has no legs, but a shaft instead. It has, however, a toe. Its toe is at the end of its face, close to its nose, which is not on its face. Although it has no body, it has a sole. It has a neck, a head, and clubs also have horns. They always have a whipping, but this has nothing to do directly with striking the ball. There is little expression in the face of a club. It is usually wooden; sometimes, however, it has a leather face. Clubs, without being clothed, occasionally have lead buttons, but never any button-holes. Clubs' heads are some black, some yellow, but colour is not due to any racial difference. From this description it will be easy to understand, without a diagram, what a club is like.

'Spoons in most respects resemble clubs. Their faces are somewhat more open. There are long, short, and mid spoons, so called according to the length of the spoon.

'Brassies differ from spoons and play clubs in that they have brass bottoms which are screwed on.

'Irons and cleeks have no sole. Their toes and noses are one and the same thing. They have iron faces. They are never whipped. They have sockets instead of necks. Their mode of locomotion is called 'approaching'. This is a short swinging gait. Sometimes, like play clubs, they drive, but no kind of club ever walks. There are different kinds of irons. A driving iron is used when it is too far to go without doing so. Lofting irons are more light-headed; they look like their work, but do not always do it. Cleeks are cleeks; they are not marked out from their creation for special uses. You may carry a driving and an approaching cleek, and a cleek for putting; but if someone steals your set, or if you die, your putting cleek may be used for driving, etc, etc.

'Then there are putters. A good one ought to have belonged to someone else before you got it – either an old golfer who is dead or else to a professional. No golfer with any self-respect uses a putter which he has bought new out of a shop for four shillings.

'The niblick is too vulgar-looking for description in a polite treatise like this. He is a good fellow, however, ever ready to get you out of a hole.

'These are the ordinary clubs, but there are many more. There are clubs with vulcanite heads, with german silver faces, with horn faces, clubs with bamboo shafts, clubs with cork grips. Old gentlemen use baffy spoons.

'The "President" is a niblick with a hole in it, which might be a very good niblick if it were not a president. It is called a president because the hole makes it clear-headed.

'There are putting irons which are not irons but putters. People who putt badly use these, and are happy, although they only put it out of their power ever to putt well. There are putters made like croquet mallets, and there are perfectly upright ones. The latter are of no use to corpulent persons, as they cannot see the ball. Even the emaciated hole out better without them.

'Old-fashioned irons look like the missing link between a meat cleaver and a kitchen spoon. They all originally belonged to somebody's grandfather, and are only now to be found in glass cases or in the sets of very bad players ... In reality, using an old-fashioned iron is the last expedient of those who cannot loft a ball with anything else. Even this expedient often fails, but defeat is at least avenged by the destruction of the green.'

Some Nifty Inventions

Sir W.G. also fancied himself as a bit of an inventor, devising little extras to help people sharpen up their game. I'll just mention three.

Automatic self-adjusting tee   This little gadget is designed to prevent toeing, heeling, topping, etc, and works rather like the compensating balance of a watch. For convenience, you are advised to 'attach the automatic tee to your button-hole by a string which can be used to lift it to your hand after each shot, just as the organ-man jerks up his monkey when about to move on.'

Putter scale   I am particularly fond of this device, and am hoping to run one up in the garage next winter. It's a light iron tripod into which you fit your putter so that the head rests just behind the ball. On the tripod is a scale showing the distance you have to draw the putter back and let it fall for each putt. Only problem is, you have to work out the length of the putt for yourself. However, with one of those builder's measuring sticks in your bag, I daresay that shouldn't take too long.

The Dynamite A very powerful weapon. Basically, it's a club with a small cartridge inserted in the face which explodes when the ball strikes it. Even the Long Hole at St Andrews can be carried in one when everything functions as it should. If you don't mind a bit of extra trouble, expense and danger, this could be the gadget for you. One final word of warning, from Sir W.G. himself: 'It would be rash to start on a round without a surgeon to carry the clubs, and surgeons of course charge more than ordinary caddies.'

Mr Uchida

In case you thought the golfing boom in Japan began suddenly in the 1960s, I have unearthed some interesting evidence that tells something of the *real* early days. That great Scottish clubmaker Tom Auchterlonie was evidently doing business with the Japanese imperial family back in the Twenties. Thanks to his son Laurie, who dug out the letters and bills, we can piece together a fascinating story.

At the heart of the dealings was Mr E.R. Uchida. We don't know much about him except that he lived in Nagasaki. Probably a whiz at import-export. Certainly, the Japanese imperial family had him squarely in their sights, and whenever one of them

wanted some new golf clubs Mr Uchida would be summoned. He'd jot down the details, and dash home to his desk to get off a letter to his contact in Scotland, a mysterious lady called Anabella, in Kirkcaldy.

'This is in hasty,' wrote Mr Uchida to Anabella on 27 June 1924, 'just to order one more set clubs for Our Imperial Family Princess Higashi Fushimi. Her age about 22, her weight 76 lbs, her height 5 feet 8 inches, and her desire is follow: *One* ivory faced Driver, *one* ivory faced Brassie, *one* light Mid Iron, *one* gigger, *one* Lofting Mashie, *one* aluminium Putter, and *one* very best light canvas bag. 6in top with hood. Put in Japanese Crest in all, same as others. Order this immediately if possible and send together in one shipment. Way to do this, you see all clubs ordered properly and after finish you examine them before you send to London Mitsui Co., as I have given you address on my last letter COD. With letter explaining to them that this is for Japanese Imperial Family. 1st go to London then by NYK steamer to Shanghai Mitsui Co., then to me then to Imperial Family. It is takes lots Red Tape but you will do for me, and be sure to charge up your Expenses on the Bill you are to send to London. I like to do this matter clean cut and business like and tell Mr Auchterlonie to be kindly make specially according to height and weight, so no mistake. They are just Beginners but they want something very nice.

We are usual. This is just in hasty.

E.R. Uchida'

Business seems to have taken off after that letter was written. In March 1925, Mr Uchida was ordering dozens of clubs, plus bags and golfing books, for sending to Japan. Some of the prices make mouth-watering reading. Princess Kuni got 8 clubs and 1 bag for £11. 8s. 0d. J. Matsuda's 10 clubs, no bag, set him back £10. 14s. 0d. H. Isao paid £9. 15s. 0d. for 7 clubs and 1 bag, and there are many other examples. Meanwhile the phrase 'just in hasty' was adopted by the Auchterlonie family for their letters to each other, and Mr Uchida seems to have achieved his ambition, expressed elsewhere, 'to get into high people'. And good luck to him.

The Old Faithfuls

The Auchterlonie workshop in St Andrews is one of those all-too-rare Aladdin's caves, a resort of wonder to addicts of the game's history – and something of a shrine to golfer-clients seeking salvation, the straight and narrow – or just an extra thirty yards. Alas, the bespoke clubmaker is an endangered breed. His is an art; only the best will do. Consequently, too few young men are prepared to risk the long toil of learning the essentials of planing, shaping, and so on, only to find that true mastery is beyond them, and that their clubs are really no better than the mass-produced lines.

It was not like that before November 1929, when the steel shaft was legitimized. One man who knows is Harry Busson. He labours still down at Walton Heath Golf Club, turning out perhaps four finely crafted clubs a week and never in danger of outpacing the waiting-list for his services. And on that waiting-list are some very great names indeed.

Up to 1930, Harry remembers, nearly all the golf professionals were clubmakers of a kind. If they were good at it, they made all the clubs to be found in their shops, even though it meant putting in almost full-time hours at the bench. Today, Harry Busson's classic woods, made of the finest persimmon, are among the most prized pieces of golfing equipment, elegant and exact in shape and 'lie', precisely honed to match an owner's needs. For the tournament professional, this usually means that the 'shape' and 'playability' are in tune with his own feelings. For the club player, it probably means that the club counter-balances an uncontrollable tendency to hook or slice, or provides loft where lack of loft has become embarrassing.

There is one type of golfer, though, who seldom treads the path to Harry's workshop. Surprisingly perhaps, it is ... a woman. Any woman. Colour of hair, shoe size, and all the statistics in between have no bearing on the matter. Woman, as a species, is not keen on investing in hand-made golf clubs.

This may be shocking, unpalatable news to some, but Harry Busson assures me it is founded on more than fifty years' professional observation of both sexes. Men, it seems, *believe* in new equipment. They reckon it's easier to buy help, in the form of a club, than have lessons and practise, which may never do the trick. Women see it differently. They take lessons, and play and practise much more than men – and remain stubbornly faithful to their old clubs, usually the first set they ever had.

Harry has no personal axe to grind – he's busy enough already – but he does take the view that golf is a more difficult game for women than for men. This being so, he feels that women 'should have all the help that the latest model clubs provide, such as carbon shafts, lightweight steel, and so on. Yet they battle on with their old has-beens!'

There was something oddly familiar about Harry's choice of phrase. Were there parallels with domestic life, I wondered? On the one side, man the hunter, darting about from one club to another, thirsting for something new to help him improve his performance. Yes, that sounds an interesting theory. On the other side is woman – less flighty, more stable and hard-working, going out doggedly in the most appalling thunderstorms to play in her Medal rounds; remaining steadfast and true to her old has-been. Old has-been?

I think, after all, we'll leave that sort of thing to the Desmond Morrises. Old has-been indeed! Good thing my wife doesn't play golf . . . .

The Miser

He hit his ball high in the air
It fell to earth he knew not where,
But when he found it in the hole
He never told a single soul.